MW01045395

Ivan Antic

EVERYTHING IS PERFECT

Why Can't We See It

SAMKHYA PUBLISHING LTD
London, 2019

Translated by
Milica Breber

Proofreading & editing by
James Joshua Pennington, PhD

Copyright © 2019 by SAMKHYA PUBLISHING LTD
All rights reserved.

ISBN: 9781688799080

CONTENT

Introduction 5

PART ONE

Why we do not see reality as perfect........................ 14
The nature of reality 27
The dimensions of nature 29
Why the unmanifested become manifested 42
How does the unmanifested become manifested 46
Consciousness, existence and the man in between ... 54
The nature of man 60
The nature of human soul is a testimony
on all the possibilities of the divine consciousness ... 69
Scientific evidence of existence of perfection 75
The perfect summary of the first part 86

PART TWO

The perfection of dying and being born 94
Sin: the perfect reason for the birth and death 103
How far are we from perfection,
or: why are people so abnormal 107
The perfection of suffering 121
Our body is perfect - Our actions spoil it 140
Causality and free will are connected perfectly 152
The perfection manifests itself
through the dialectics of oppositions 163
The dialectics of life and death 170
The dialectics of success and failure 180
Karmic maturity and the circling
of divine consciousness 189
How to overcome oppositions 199
The perfection of spiritual practice 213
Shiva's advice for recognizing perfection 224
How can we be perfect 243

INTRODUCTION

This description of the perfection of everything must begin with a minor introduction where I reveal how the inspiration for this kind of writing came about. Two events that took place not too far apart within the space of several years, largely contributed to the occurrence of this book. Those events, each in its own way, did not play a crucial role in the origin of the material before your eyes. They were merely factors that grouped together all the experiences of my life, connecting into a meaningful whole the previously seemingly unconnected parts, hence setting in motion my inspiration.

The first event occurred three days after the death of my mother, Angelia Antic. She, with my ability for recognizing the true nature of a human soul, can be placed in that category of souls, which Michael Newton, in his book "Journey of Souls" describes as "masters" or "wise beings", who represent souls that have reached the state of overcoming the reincarnation cycles and who choose to enter a physical body for the sole purpose of helping a fellow soul. That other soul, in this case, was me. She was my guide, protector and teacher. She showed me, with her actions and her being, all the intricacies and qualities which the greatest souls in this world possess. My other helper was Bhagavan Sri Ramana Maharshi. He came to me a long time ago in a dream, before I even knew who he was and that he existed in this world, and with brief meditation instructions, he taught me how to awaken from my dreams that existed in the real world. Subsequently, I found out that my mother and Ramana Maharshi were connected on the planes of existence that far surpass the realms of the physical world.

The first event happened three days after the physical death of my mother. I was very interested to know to where her soul departed after death. This wish of mine had most likely drawn her attention, for she contacted me soon afterward. The "deceased" often do that to their dear ones in order to comfort them, but "the living" rarely recognize their communication. It was easy for me to see that instantly, because that morning, I had with full awareness found myself on the astral plane, out of the body. Previously I had had many out-of-body experiences, so that was not an unusual state for me; quite the opposite, it was perfectly normal. I saw my mother. She looked much younger than her age when she "died", exactly the way she looked in her most beautiful years. I asked her how she was doing. She only replied: "Everything is perfect". At that moment I also saw all the contents of her response, something which is possible on the astral plane primarily, because in those higher dimensions time and space are contracted, one can see in a timeless moment everything that words cannot begin to express. I saw all the key events of my life as parts of a perfect whole which is not segmented in time, but rather as a perfect, logical unity and harmony. In all likelihood, what she had said did not apply to herself only, that everything was perfect for her, she rather meant the whole existence is perfect; that nothing can be different; and that we are neither separate nor different from the perfection of the whole. We can only dream that we are apart, and that dream represents this physical life we have in reality, and together with it all our lives, all our misconceptions and all the suffering ultimately belong to that dream, although in reality we cannot be separated from the timeless whole that represents perfection.

The second event complemented the first one in an extraordinary way. I have always had good communication with trees. Communication with trees does not consist of words, of course; rather its done through images, visions and feelings. When a tree tells you something, then it spills out everything it has in the form of one picture and in one direct insight. In other words, it communicates on a higher dimension than that of the physical one, on which all things are separate. It uses a dimension in which everything is connected as one. Therefore, in order to communicate with trees, you need to be open to those higher dimensions. The openness for higher dimensions was not unknown to me, because I have, owing to the practice of meditation, entered them with full alertness during my out-of-body experiences. When you go often enough, it is as though you are digging out a passageway or a kind of a channel – a conduit for information. By using those open channels, communication with plants becomes possible. One day, during my usual stroll through the forest I saw a clearing with a solitary old oak tree standing in the middle. It grew symmetrically and unperturbed from all sides, which only made it more appealing, attracting attention with its beautiful foliage. The trees which grow in the midst of the forest must learn to adapt to each other, so they predominantly grow in height, in an attempt to reach the sunlight, not achieving the harmonious potential like this solitary oak tree.

I approached the oak tree, placed my hand on the bark and felt its old age and its way of living. Suddenly, it dawned on me to me to ask the oak what kind of a life it had had since it is sits immobile, living in a single spot only, and whether a life like this would lead to boredom. A powerful answer followed. I received a clear vision of its perception, of the way in which that tree perceives life, and how, in accordance with this, it experiences existence itself, in such a way that any form of movement is practically redundant.

All life is shaped in accordance with the perception of consciousness. I saw clearly that one same divine consciousness transforms itself into everything that exists, into the cosmos itself and life. It turns into mineral shapes with which it experiences its existence in every possible inert form, in the shape of the element. It turns into the plant world which, apart from its physical form, also has perception, but lacks movement. It turns into the animal form, which, apart from the shape of perception, is in possession of the physical movement, as well, with which it experiences all the possibilities of perception, to a far higher degree than plants do. Animals, through the food chain, perfect their movement and perception (a predator develops senses and movements in order to hunt the prey down, and prey does the same to save itself). In its final expression, the divine consciousness is also manifested in the human, who apart from perception and movement also possesses the psychological drama of life, the substance of life with which they experience the meaning of all possible phenomena. The human has karma and the option to create a variety of new experiences and contents, shapes, not merely for the purpose of perceiving the already existing life passively. Through human self-consciousness, the perception of existence is completely realized upon recognizing the true meaning of existence. At that point, the human has awakened to the divine consciousness of everything, which means that the divine consciousness has returned to itself then, enriched, not only by manifesting itself in the human, but also by perceiving itself through the human who is its conscious subject. After having been enriched by all the possibilities of action through an awaken man first.

That tree showed me that there is no fallacy or lack of any kind – everything is perfect, as my mother said. The divine consciousness is neither lost nor does it suffer any form of limitation. It simply exists, there is no multitude of different types of consciousnesses, only one exists as the basis for the entire nature that gets expressed in all possible ways, through all the individual shapes. In minerals, it is completely open to itself. The elements are on their quantum level and completely connected into one, all subatomic particles are interconnected and they are constantly communicating, that is, they are all fully aware of one another, independent of space and time. They could be thousands of miles apart and they would still react and communicate as if they were together. Plants are close to minerals and for this reason they are the first in line through which the divine consciousness creates new shapes that are above simple elements, and sets itself into motion. Plants possess the ability to move, albeit minimally; but this is sufficient for their immediate survival.

However, the oak conveyed to me that there is no loss, for although it is compelled to live in one spot its entire life, for centuries even, it has the ability to perceive the entire universe. Plants react to distant cosmic events, cosmic radiations, explosions of supernova, they perceive all feelings and states of consciousness of each living being that enter their surroundings. However, the oak tree failed to tell me whether it perceives the states and feelings of all living beings on this planet simultaneously, although it would not come as a surprise to me. Therefore, there is no real need for the oak tree to move around and gather experiences in such a way, in a manner that we people do. It is already in possession of all the experiences that it is able to detect from the environment, all our experiences are its experiences, too. Its perception is in direct reverse proportion to its movements. Animals suffer no loss for their inability to speak or act the way people do, because they generally perceive more than people, they see auras, states and feelings of other beings, they understand everything you tell them even though they cannot speak the language. They do not need books to know what to do to make you laugh, make your day, and engage in saving lives at times. Since human perception is blocked off we must be in motion and do stuff in order to learn and grow. Likewise, human perception is in reverse proportion to his movement and action. That is why the human must quieten himself in meditation in order to expand perception completely. There are many reasons that justify this, man can experience many things that plants and animals cannot. However, that oak tree is evidently not bored for the lack of movement and suffering that people go through; the suffering which also falls under the category of mandatory experiences of the divine consciousness.

The calmness of plants has a soothing effect on us for one very simple reason – they are grounded in existence far better than we are, their sensitivity exceeds that of ours by far. That is the key reason why we love plants. With their calmness they transmit tous the things we truly need, but have difficulty recognizing as such: namely, that existence itself is self-sufficient, self-containing and ever-present, which is something we finally come to realize after a long cycle of reincarnation and all our gathered experience as the final result. We are attracted to plants for their inner ability to simply enjoy life, existence; they are deeply rooted in the soil and completely open to the sky doing nothing much more than that. This way, they achieve everything. They act without acting; action without exertion is the central principle of TAO (*wu wei*). They connect the sky to the earth, they are able to convey the highest vibrations of the cosmos onto the physical reality of earth. For this reason, they are our staple food, not only in the nutritive sense, but our soul food, as well. Anatomically, man was designed to be a fruit-eater.

We are attracted to animals in a similar way, because of their unity with existence. Every animal is always only what it is, acting in accordance with its own nature, with its entire being; it can never be fake. That is how animals connect us to existence itself. Existence shows us how to move, rejoice, wag our tails and play; and, moreover, how to fight for our basic survival when the opportunity arises, despite all limitations. Most wild animals are, as an inherent part of nature, cruelly simplistic in their struggle for survival. However, those few animals that live with us, or beside us, can convey all the purity of consciousness of the divine soul due to the clarity of their own nature and their connectedness to existence. Before it reaches human form, the divine consciousness is expressed in its most superior degree in animals.

Consequently, I would like to add one more experience to complement this story which took place not long after the incidence of my psychotherapy with the oak. I had a Zen Koan with a raven. One morning, upon leaving my house, I saw a small raven on the ground, standing by the wall. Then, I heard a creepy sound above my head, the frequency of which gave me goose bumps. I saw two big black wings above my head and felt the touch of soft feathers on top of my head. That was the raven's father. I saw another raven flying in circles above me which turned out to be his mother. They were protecting their little one who fell out of the nest in an attempt to fly. They protected him by warning me not to touch their little one in a way that crashes Darwin's theory of the evolution of species, which is still thrown at us today, even though the real place for this theory would be the junkyard of history, where it belongs. He figured out in a flash how to go about it. He did not attack me, because he saw I was bigger and stronger and I could hurt him and his offspring – it could even have plucked my hair like the scene in a Hitchcock movie.[1] Instead, gently using his stomach only, the softest part of his body, touched the top of my head with perfect precision. His feet did not touch my head even. That was all. And that was all it took. One moment of perfection. He had managed to come up with all of that in an instant despite his pea-sized brain. It took me the whole day, and quite a bit of processing, to comprehend the perfection of that event. The additional help was that I knew ravens have the ability to produce around 800 different sounds in their mutual communication, and are also capable of using tools. Their young live with their parents for about ten years before finally learning everything that is needed for life, so that they can safeguard and help each other later on. They can do this without having a big brain, for consciousness that fills their entire being is at the base of the entire nature, and the entire existence.

---

[1] Alfred Hitchcock: The Birds (1963).

The perfection of existence is predicated on this consciousness.

We shall depict that perfection from the human point of view here, because it seems that people are the only ones who need that. They are deprived of perceiving that perfection more than anyone else in existence. That is why they create this kind of chaos in the world.

Each one of you has felt that perfection, even while observing a bird sitting on a tree. In this introduction I have already disclosed some other dimensions to you, the unexpected realms of the birds and trees. I try to inspire you to feel the same and look for them in other aspects of existence.

The perfection of the divine consciousness that conditions everything is always there. We only need a little stirring up to remind ourselves of it, some detachment from illusions in order to be able to observe it in everything, at any given moment.

PART ONE

WHY WE DO NOT SEE REALITY AS PERFECT

We certainly do not experience reality as perfect, we rather view it as the battlefield of different influences that are beyond our control. At times these are a source of great suffering which appears so unfair to us, whilst at the same time we make the extra effort to be good and consequently, we would do good unto others as we would like to be done unto us. Therefore, it presents a great challenge to claim the otherwise, and that is that everything is perfect. All challenges can be resolved by understanding, and in this particular instance by understanding the nature of reality, human nature and the nature of consciousness.

Our initial point must begin at the basic logic of this conundrum. If existence were not already perfect, life, as such, would not prevail. Even though phenomena that seem imperfect exist, there would not be a way out of them, problems and disagreements would be common and unsolvable were the imperfection at the base of everything. There would be no development and growth if perfection were not at the base. The destructiveness would collapse into itself. We see this is not the case, things keep developing, a way out of the worst situation can be found, although illogical and destructive phenomena do occur, gradually over a period of time, they are upgraded and harmonized, thus functionally overcome. No positive outcome would be an option, were it not for the already existing perfection as the starting point.

Something cannot come out of nothing, but rather it comes out of something concrete that was originally perfect. Therefore, imperfect phenomena would not be possible if at the basis of everything were not perfection. *They are only local phenomena that occur in time and space of the timeless whole that is in its essence perfect.* Neither would perfection be so desirable if it were, continually, monotonous and impersonal, without the shadows that are necessary to bring out the light. It seems that all imperfect phenomena exist only for us with the aim of raising our awareness of the perfection.

The reason why we do not see the perfection of reality is simply due to the fact that we do not see the entire reality, we remain unaware of the fact that existence has multiple dimensions. We do not see all the dimensions of nature, merely its roughest, physical phenomenon, the one which we are able to perceive with our senses. However, physical phenomenon is only the final outcome of the previous causes and processes that have a much finer structure than that of the physical world, hence our failure to perceive them. Sometimes we feel and suspect that there is something more than this, but it all remains unclear. Sometimes we even experience something "extrasensory", but only for a short time and without understanding the full context, either our own or other people's. Science has discovered that with our senses we are able to perceive only 5% of the entire nature, and the remaining 95%, which exist only in the form of physical reality, we are unable to perceive. Besides such physical reality that we cannot see in its entirety, other dimensions of reality are equally present. We can only see them in our dreams, but we can also dream of them.

The perfection of existence is predicated on three logical facts only:

- the essence of existence itself;
- on causality; and
- on purposefulness.

The essence of existence in general, and the one of the cosmos and nature, is such that it cannot exist unless it were perfect and comprehensive. Nothing wrong can exist. Therefore, only existence must be perfect at every single moment, exactly the way it is or, otherwise, it could not exist.

The other logical foundation for perfection is causality. Nothing can exist without a cause. Nothing cannot generate anything, something must come out of something (the teleological argument). The perfection of existence is based on causality. Causality is based on the holographic unity of all the factors of existence, on the fundamental unity of everything. Holographic connectedness and unity are based on the perfection of everything. This is a closed circle that constitutes the perfection of everything. The model of the hologram is best depicted in the subatomic, quantum reality, where everything is interconnected with everything else, everything is oneness and oneness is everything. That is the fundamental reality of existence.

The third fact is the purposefulness of existence. All causes have a purpose. Therefore, existence itself possesses a purpose. Unlike the causality that is manifested through concrete shapes and events, the purpose refers to the meaning, to the world of ideas and cognition, as the purpose of existence unravels in man, in his consciousness and self-knowing, in understanding. The causality manifests itself through the entire nature and its laws, and the purpose reveals itself in the most conscious subject of all existence, in the human, and their making sense of the essence of existence and the overall understanding. Thus the whole is made complete.

Once we are able to see the cause, all phenomena become logical and clear. However, nature consists of far more dimensions that we are able to perceive with our senses. We are usually witnesses to the lowest one, the material reality. Causality in nature spans all the dimensions. We only see the lowest one, the one where the process of causality brings forth the consequences. Even on this physical plane, limited by space and time, we do not see all the consequences, merely segments of them. The starting point of the process of causality takes place in higher dimensions that are off limits to our ordinary senses. Being unable to follow through the entire process of causality and the accompanying consequences, many things appear out of touch with reality to us, without the obvious connection of the opposing factors, a stroke of luck and coincidence or, conversely, great injustice and evil doing.

That would be the first and the most important reason why we do not perceive the perfection of everything: we do not see all of reality, merely parts of it.

Why do we fail to see all of reality? We do not see the reality in its entirety because our own being remains hidden away from us, too. We do not know the stuff we are made of. *Only to the degree we become aware of the reality of our own being, we can become aware of the reality of existence itself.* The reality is the same as we are. The one who observes must indeed be suitable to observe. The reason for this lies in the holographic nature of the universe. Universe is such that each piece contains within itself the framework of the whole. That is why the one who observes in the holographic universe, is no different from what is observed. If our perception were not perfect and complete per se, then what we perceive could not be perfect and complete, either. The subject and the object are, by no means, a separate phenomenon in reality. If they appear separate, it is only due to the illusion. And that illusion is the only problem which we shall unveil here.

It is not very realistic to assume that we can know the nature of reality if we do not know our own true nature. We do our reasoning only based on the conscious mind that we use when we are awake. Apart from it, we are also in possession of the unconscious mind, and the higher mind. Psychology has discovered merely tiny fragments of their relationship between one another and the impact it has on our lives. They are far greater and stronger that the conscious mind. However, this minute conscious mind that we are using as we speak, is not the only one, because it has multiple centers. It keeps changing, perpetually adjusting itself to every moment and satisfying the current needs. We do not have one I, but a multitude of I's. Such a mind is not even designed to recognize the highest reality, its task is only to govern the senses and perception, and to maintain control over the body. It is like a charioteer who has never left his village. The horses represent the senses and the carriage is the body. The mind/ego is the driver. It will not do to expect of it to be an astronaut. It does not have the right qualifications. For this very reason, all spiritual teachings require discipline and quietness of the mind, in order for people to be able to become aware of the contents of higher reality. The true realization of the true nature of reality starts only with the discipline of restraint of the self-willfulness of the mind with the aim of annulling its influence, and preferably, overcoming it permanently. Only then, the presence of the consciousness of the soul, the divine consciousness sitting at the base of all existence, will disclose itself to us.

This is the main reason why we do not see the reality as perfect. It is within us.

In nature, nothing is separate, the entire nature is one unique whole, one living being. Higher dimensions are also an integral part of our being that we, mostly, are unaware of, since we focus all our attention on the physical observation. The science of yoga, namely meditation (Patanjali's *Yoga Sutras*) bring awareness to our entire being in a systematic way so that we can become aware of the higher dimensions of nature, in order to see reality at its fullest.

Only then, when we become aware of our entire being, we can become aware of the fact that the entire existence is a positive phenomenon. Actually, nothing negative exists. Everything that exists is beneficial, the only question is whether we see it as a complete phenomenon in all the dimensions, or only a fragment of it so that it seems illogical or negative to us, for our lack of understanding.

Always when we see the whole, we see everything positive.

Always when we experience something as negative, that means we do not see the whole.

In order to see everything as perfect, we need to see the entire nature. There are forces of deception that trick us into believing that is not possible (materialistic science teaches us that we are the product of chance, genetic error, that our origin can be traced back to the monkeys... and religions make it their business to convince us that because of our ancestral sin we know nothing and "only God knows everything" etc..). We are able to see the entire nature, because human being is the embodiment and the reflection of the entire nature, man is a microcosm in its most supreme form, all the principles of cosmos are reflected in every human being. Actually, everything is the reflection of the whole. Each element of the cosmos is a microcosm. Man falls under the category of the microcosm because the whole universe is a hologram. Nothing is separate and everything is contained within everything. That means that the path to perception of perfection of the nature of existence leads through self-realization, through our perfection. It does not lead into the outside world, but it leads within. *Our perception of the world the way it really is, as the perfect one, will never be possible for us until we learn to be perfect in the perception of ourselves and in all our deeds.*

Our perception, consciousness and action are not divided because of the holographic nature of existence. We do not see the holographic nature of existence, because of the fact that our perception, consciousness and actions have been divided.

This is the issue of the openness to perception. The wholeness of the most supreme reality is already here and now, everything consists of it and in order for us to perceive it, we only need to open ourselves to it, the way plants and the rest of nature opens to it. All sages point in that direction, toward the openness, the cessation of closing ourselves off into the mind and ego, which function in terms of sensory and bodily perception only. All religions base their teaching on the supernatural. However, they also carry the seed of deception in that the man is incapable of perceiving everything, his role in life is to be the servant to God and his slave, that he only needs to succumb to a higher force. Such convictions drove a wedge between us and the whole, away from the holographic existence, they are one of the real reasons why we do not see the divine perfection in everything as well as in ourselves. Those are illusions in which we have lived (*maya*) throughout our entire history. ***Our entire history is actually the harmonization between our perception, consciousness and action.*** That harmonization creates culture and civilization. When perception, consciousness and action become one, meaning well-harmonized in all the dimensions of our being one day, this world will be heaven. It already is, but first and foremost, man must make a quantum leap within his being and return to this world consciously, learn to recognize it, be worthy of it by means of: perception, consciousness and action.

In order to understand the perfection of existence in all its dimensions, we need to acquaint ourselves with the basic principles of existence. There are several of them.

- The nature of the Absolute is such that it manifests into the multitude of phenomena, such as the nature and cosmos, and the world which is visible to us, but also the world beyond.

- The Absolute is manifested in all the possible phenomena with the purpose of experiencing all the options of its own existence, and all the discrepancies. ***The Absolute, who is the all-that-is, is manifested as everything-that-could-be.*** The Absolute, in the form of nature, manifests itself into a variety of the subatomic, atomic, molecular, mineral and biological shapes. The same manifestation is also reflected in human experience, since our early childhood and all along the life path, people experience everything they possibly can. Young children are prone to minor injuries, a bruised knee or broken bone that could also be a part of the learning process. However, in adult people, experience also results from assorted historical events tied together with the development of civilization, which are often followed by an even greater degree of destruction. All of those are experiences of everything-that-is being manifested as everything-that-could-be.

The Absolute becomes manifested because the nature of the Absolute is pure consciousness, and the consciousness is the perception and self-awareness in its most refined form. Therefore, the Absolute represents the perception and the self-awareness in itself. It manifests itself into all the possibilities that could ever exist only for the sake of its own perception and self-knowing. We would not do it justice by commencing a philosophical debate on the subject of the Absolute here, if it already represents in its own nature the awareness of itself, there is no need for it to be aware of itself, to be what it truly is. The nature of the consciousness itself is the perception and the self-awareness and that is why this needs to happen, it needs to manifest itself. Absolute must be manifested into something that can be observed, and, understandably, into all the possible phenomena, so that its consciousness could reach the level of awareness of itself, in order to have something to observe and perceive. It could be said that the Absolute is a stick, and the subject and the object are two ends of the stick. In that sense, the subject and the object are connected. The nature of consciousness acts in a way of manifesting itself for the purpose of reflecting itself to itself. Without that manifestation, the Absolute is, in itself, a void. Hence, both are true: a statement that the Absolute is essentially without attributes, self-sufficient and complete in itself, and that it is a void without conditioning, (sunyata) as the Buddhists and some mystics see it, as *purusha* in *sânkhya* - but also that it is manifested in this form of our rough reality full of contradiction, filled with all kinds of context (prakrti).

Our reality is a way in which the Absolute exists. *The cosmos is the mirror in which the consciousness of the Absolute reflects itself to itself.* The cosmos cannot be anything but this, it has no other function aside from this. It is important to keep this always in mind. The cosmos is nothing but a hologram. If it were not like this, it could not exist. The final conclusion is *that all the phenomena take place within the Absolute itself; there could be nothing outside of it, because that would go against its nature*, it would not be the Absolute, whole, complete and universal.

- The way in which the Absolute tests all the possibilities of existence, that is, all the opposites, is through the process of individualization of consciousness of the Absolute into individual souls, the monads. They are the first emanations of the Absolute, its first manifestations. In religions, they are picturesquely described as its archangels and angels.

- The manifested monads of consciousness, the souls, create all other shapes of existence, the entire cosmos, mineral, plant, animal and human world.

- To experience the finest form of existence, the human existence, through which the consciousness will reach a sense of existence and thus return to the Absolute as the awareness of itself, the consciousness of the souls is further divided into smaller individual souls, that are incarnated in human form many times over which represents the incarnation cycles of human souls which constitutes all our living.

That is the way in which consciousness of the divine Absolute matures throughout the process of acquiring experience of all the possibilities by means of individuation of consciousness, from the projection of the cosmos itself down to human incarnations with the goal of experiencing all the opposites, all the possible states of consciousness and the shapes of existence. There is no fundamental separation and contradiction between good and bad experiences, all of them are intricately connected; only experiences as such exist.

Human experiences are the finest experiences that underly the meaning of existence. The divine consciousness that is limited and trapped in the: human body, mind and ego, is the farthest and the finest point of manifestation of the divine consciousness into its exact opposite state. Thus, the human mind maintains the illusion of separation from God and from all of nature. That is the highest peak of illusion of creation committed by the divine consciousness. After this experience, the only remaining thing to do is to return to the divine consciousness.

That highest peak of illusion reflected in human experience is expressed so beautifully in the Gospels with the crucifixion of the "Son of man" and his loud cry "My God, my God, why hast thou forsaken me?" (Matthew 27:46). That is the darkest hour, the experience when the mind and the ego are completely cut off from the divine whole. Every human goes through this experience. That is an illusory moment because nothing could exist outside the divine whole. However, this is also the climax and the ultimate reach of the creation of everything – the manifestation of the divine consciousness in the form of cosmos. The peak of the illusion of the Whole lies within itself. If we imagine the whole as a circle or sphere (Tai Chi, the symbol of the circulation of yin and yang; more on this later, in the final chapter), which is the only correct image, it represents the farthest, the most distant point of cyclicity. Upon reaching this ultimate, opposing, point in the manifestation of consciousness, the return of the divine consciousness to itself follows suit. This return happens in the human, as self-realization or god-realization. When the consciousness of the divine Absolute reaches itself in that furthest aspect of the self, in the human body, then it has come to the end of its manifestation, and begins to return to itself. That particular human has recognized the divine consciousness in themselves. This is how the third fact of the perfection of existence gets fulfilled - purposefulness in raising awareness of the meaning of life.

All of that is nicely described in the Gospels, where, after the cry of abandonment, the reconciliation and the return to the divine follow: "Father, into your hands I surrender my spirit" (Luke, 23:46).[2]

We have one same consciousness in everything, all the way from the divine Absolute, who uses a mirror for self-realization as the cosmos itself, down to our every thought, and every cognition that use our body and our actions as the mirror. In our thoughts, cosmos can be

---

[2] That moment of ultimate surrender is expressed in musical works also, not only in the numerous written materials and books. J.S. Bach, at the end of his life, literally on his death bed, dictated the notes of the choral prelude "Before Thy Throne I Now Appear" to his son (Wenn wir in hochsten Nöten sein), that is found at the end of his "The Art of Fugue" (Bach, J. S.: The Art of Fugue; A Musical Offering (2 CDs), Stuttgarter Kammerorchester and Karl Münchinger. The best performer is (the piano interpretation) Charles Rosen. Bach's "The art of Fugue" is the science of the perfect circling of the whole. *Fugare* means "recurrence", one theme begins and then it is repeated in all possible versions making it an integrated whole – in its essence it is actually holographic music, because the vibrations represent the golden section, vibrations of the whole translated into music. J.S. Bach always said that he did not compose the music, but only jotted down the perfect harmony that comes from God in the form of musical notes. All his musical pieces are devoted to God.

known down to the finest detail, and only on that spot can everything be connected in one meaningful whole.

The same way in which cosmos is a mirror for self-realization of the Absolute consciousness of itself, the same way our body and actions act as a mirror for self-realization of our individual consciousness of itself.

When an individual soul which is in the body becomes aware of what potentials for action there are, and realizes what their true meaning is, at that breaking point consciousness returns to the divine Absolute as its awareness of itself. When it receives awareness of the finest aspects of existence, through the human experience of existence, the odyssey of consciousness through existence is finalized at long last. At that moment, the consciousness of the Absolute is actualized in all the possibilities of existence. From that point onward, the issue is about actualization only and nothing else, for everything that already exists in the absolute sense aspires to be actualized into all the possibilities concretely. In human experience it happens as self-realization which is in reality God-realization, or the most supreme form of enlightenment.

Consequently, nothing has happened outside the divine Absolute, because its nature is such that nothing is even possible outside it. Yet again, it has actualized itself, everything that could and should have happened finally happened. Fundamentally, there is no difference between the unmanifested and the manifested Absolute.

THE NATURE OF REALITY

The nature of reality is divided into the manifested and unmanifested.

The most supreme one which is the source of everything has always been called the divine, God, and here we call it the unmanifested Absolute. It is without attributes, which means it cannot be known. It is present in religious experiences, such as apophatic theology in Christianity, and sunyata, or emptiness in Buddhism. It also goes by the name of *purusha* in *sâmkhya*. Its nature is transcendental, which means that it overcomes any mental concepts.

The unmanifested nature of reality in recent times has been defined by physicists, as the universal quantum field, the field from which all elementary particles that constitute atoms originate. It exists and acts as the unmanifested field where all that we see in our rough material world as manifested is already present. The quantum field exists as the hidden or implicit order in our revealed or explicit world we live in[3]. Within it, all possibilities are already present, which will in accordance with the circumstances, allow them to be manifested into the visible world, as some shape or phenomenon, an event.

---

[3] David Bohm – Wholeness And The Implicate Order (First published 1980 by Routledge & Kegan Paul)

It has been proven experimentally that this sub-atomic world of the quantum field operates irrelevant of space and time, that everything is interconnected within it, that information from all subatomic particles is instantly transmitted from one to another, even though they are far apart in space. In other words, in this quantum field which acts as the foundation of the natural reality, everything is connected in an inseparable whole, beyond the category of space and time. The nature is at its basis an entire Whole, without any partitions.

In accordance with this, it has been discovered that the nature of reality corresponds to that of the hologram. Thus, the theory of the holographic universe was created, the one that states that everything in the cosmos is connected in a similar way to that of the hologram where each piece contains the image of the whole.[4]

---

[4] On the universal field in contemporary physics, see the book Lynne McTaggart: *The Field: The Quest for the Secret Force of the Universe* (2003). On the holographic paradigm see in the book of Michael Talbot: *The Holographic Universe*, 1991. For further understanding and the connection of the consciousness and quantum field with the holographic universe see the work of Gregg Braden: *The Divine Matrix: Bridging Time, Space, Miracles, and Belief*, 2006.

THE DIMENSIONS OF NATURE

The manifested reality is the entire cosmos, and not only the physical world we are able to perceive with our senses and mind. Reality is manifested across several dimensions. The dimensions of nature are represented with the elements of, air, fire, water and earth, in esoteric science of the East and West. We will show the pyramid structure of them, for easier understanding.

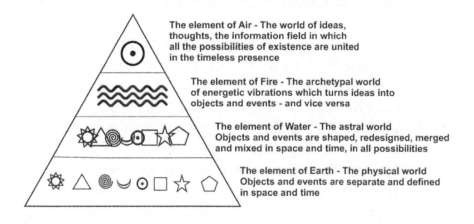

The element of Air - The world of ideas, thoughts, the information field in which all the possibilities of existence are united in the timeless presence

The element of Fire - The archetypal world of energetic vibrations which turns ideas into objects and events - and vice versa

The element of Water - The astral world Objects and events are shaped, redesigned, merged and mixed in space and time, in all possibilities

The element of Earth - The physical world Objects and events are separate and defined in space and time

Picture 1

Beyond all the dimensions is ether or *akasha*, which is also known as the quantum field in contemporary physics. That is the area of pure consciousness that is the closest in its qualities to the unmanifested Absolute. It is the absolute awareness of itself, outside space and time, which means it is timeless. It is above all the dimensions.

All dimensions are merely processes of manifestation, from the finest to the roughest. *Akasha* or ether, represent the quantum field which is unmanifested.

Underneath *akasha* is the element of air. That is the dimension in which the divine consciousness, for the first time, starts to manifest itself as cosmos. At the base of the entire cosmos is pure consciousness, the information field. The first act of manifestation of consciousness is information[5]. It is visible as the creative force that formed the entire nature. All creations of nature were created by means of intelligent design. In man, that is the world of ideas and thoughts, the ability to see and interpret all the manifestations that take place in nature in all the possible ways, independently of space and time, to devise and implement them for the sake of understanding and doing impeccable deeds.

Beneath that is the element of fire. There, the ideas begin, for the first time, to act in a specific manner, to show their strength and first shapes, and to vibrate in one direction. They are no longer abstract ideas, but intention or the will for realization. It is the world of energy. Here, information becomes a force that exerts.

Beneath that is the element of water. Here, the conscious intention created with an idea has taken on a concrete form in imagination. There, the idea has nothing abstract about it anymore, but it becomes a concrete shape, with all the details, however still not physical.

The element of earth comes in the end, and there the idea (the air) which has through the intention and will (fire) perfected its shape (water) has become a concrete physical phenomenon (earth).

---

[5] Logos. In the beginning was the Word, and the Word was with God, and the Word was God. All things were made by him." John 1. 1-3

That is how everything is manifested into existence.

All the dimensions of nature are only different vibrations of the same particle.

That single particle, here we will call "the divine particle" (without any religious connotations).[6]

The "divine particle" comes into existence as the first and foremost manifestation of the divine consciousness of the Absolute. Namely, the divine consciousness of the Absolute is manifested as the entire cosmos, but it is under no obligation to do that in the form of a multitude of things and phenomena, molecules, beings and objects. That would be too big of a job. Actually, that would be mission impossible. All of that happens in a much simpler manner. Since the divine Absolute is outside space and time, it is enough for it to manifest itself as its exact opposite, and that is the "divine particle".

If we display the Absolute in the form of a circle, its counter reflection is the point in the middle of that circle. That point is the "divine particle". The entire manifestation of the divine Absolute has been finalized with this act. However, that point, the "divine particle" contains within itself all the properties of the divine Absolute, which means that it is also timeless and spaceless. That practically means that it becomes manifested irrelevant of space and time. More accurately put: it manifests the entire space within the boundaries of time, all of existence, because existence does not exist without the inter-

---

[6] The phrase we use here, the divine particle, has nothing in common with the book: *The God Particle*, a popular science book by Leon M. Lederman and Dick Teresi, published in 1993. It is mainstream science. Here the divine particle is like a point in Euclidean geometry, which has no dimensional properties, but it possesses all the properties of the Absolute.

vention of the divine Absolute. That "divine particle" manifests space and time by vibrating currently, much faster than the speed of light, in accordance with the patterns of fractal geometry and golden section, creating all the other phenomena with its vibrations, which we, here in the rough physical world, perceive as the multitude of particles, which create a multitude of atoms, which again create a multitude of elements, which further create a multitude of molecules, which, in the final outcome, create all the beings and all the phenomena on the plane of this physical reality.

All that exists vibrates and this vibration, in its essence, it is energy. Therefore, all the subatomic particles, according to the laws of quantum physics, can be reduced to pure energy, in their finest state they disappear as special particles and only energy remains. To sum up, the *omnipresent energy in nature comes from the vibration of "the divine particle"*.

Why does "the divine particle" vibrate? Because, every single moment it keeps returning from its manifested state into the unmanifested one. In other words, the divine Absolute itself vibrates like that, every moment it turns into its opposition, and manifests itself as "the divine particle", and at the same time it once again goes back to its unmanifested state. That return happens in every single timeless moment. Actually, each moment is made up of that return back to the original unmanifested state, and the manifestation into the "divine particle", which is instantly manifested in the form of universe. That is possible because the divine reality is one timeless present, and presence also. In that way, the divine Absolute is present in everything both as the consciousness and as energy, as the vibration, and all of it takes place following a pattern of the holographic model.

Vibration is information at the same time, acting similarly to the way in which in electromagnetism a vibration turns into information, vibrating into its opposite, between 1 and 0, the same way the "divine particle" vibrates from its unmanifested into the manifested state, and those vibrations are never identical following the set model of fractal geometry and shaping absolutely everything that can be shaped in the process. Vibration is information because it is the bearer of consciousness of the divine Absolute itself. Therefore, consciousness is at the base of the entire cosmos, everything is the intelligent design. Consciousness is under no obligation to travel using a medium of any kind; it is independent of space and time. The same works for energy. It is not transmitted and it does not engage in travel, it is at the base of everything. Many resources would be required if the energy and consciousness had to travel across space and time. Physics has proven to be the foundations of all the phenomena of the finest quantum field. In fact, the cosmos would not be able to function at all if the energy and consciousness were not omnipresent, if they had to cross countless miles to get transmitted.

To use the parabola of Guadapada, the teacher of Adi Shankara, who taught *advaita vedanta*. The action of "the divine particle" is similar to the torch being swung about fast forming a fire circle. Even though to us it appears a solid whole, it is actually only one point of light that is moving fast. In the same way, the "divine particle" moves so fast, much faster than light, currently to be exact, because at its divine base, everything is timeless, so much so that here, we see its vibrations as a multitude of particles, a multitude of compact things and phenomena. In that way, at the base of the entire cosmos only one particle exists. All of us are that particle, we are together with all the stars made up of one divine element. Your body is made up of the same particle as all the other bodies that you see around you, and the ones that remain invisible to us, and the entire nature is, consequently, comprised of the same. That is the essence of *advaita vedanta*, the teaching that there is no duality or multitude, that everything is one, and that One is *Brahman*, the divine Absolute, and it is also our *Atman*, our soul. Those are not parabolas, that is literally One. That is the essential message all saints try to convey to us, they recognized God in themselves, which has enabled them to see God in everything. Nothing else exists but the divine Absolute, it is the only reality.

The story of the "divine particle" originates from the cosmology of the ancient Slav-Aryan Vedas. They were taken to the south a long time ago, to the Indian subcontinent where they underwent a certain modification, but are still known to us as Vedas even today. The truth is that the Indian interpretation of Vedas is false. According to this cosmology, the entire universe is created from one point-seed, (*bindu*), which spreads throughout many eons, the *yugas* (millions of years) and *kalpas* (billion of years), *Brahmas years* (3 trillion, 110 billion, 400 million earth years), a very long period of time and once again returns into its original unmanifested state, figuratively represented as the seed, *bindu*, or point. This story of the unimaginably long period of time during which cosmos manifests itself from one point into the entire universe as the first step, and returns again into its original state of a single point as the final step, is the story for people who are identified with the mind which projects the illusion of time. That is largely a falsified story.

According to the original lore of the Slav-Aryan Vedas, all of this keeps on happening within a timeless reality each and every moment, all the cosmos is projected from one point and into the universe and on its way back, it returns to its original point every single second. There are no *kalpas* or "days of Brahma" or "Brahma's years" to speak of.

Every single moment consists of that vibration.

Everything that exist consists of that vibration.

Since each moment is the same way, it is timeless.

Since it becomes manifested the way it does, there are both - the time and the timeless present. That is why time always rests on the timeless present. All the realities coexist in parallel. We can be aware of both, of the time and of the timeless present. The more we are aware of the timeless present, the more we are aware of everything in time. The more we are identified with time, the less we are aware of the timeless present, and the reality as it is, and the more we are trapped in illusion and suffering.

None of this has to be so abstract. We can understand all of this in one very simple and practical way.

Observe the thing you have in your hand, in your surroundings, feel the air that you breathe, the ground you stand on. It is all matter, it exists in the solid, liquid, vibrational and gaseous state. If you are aware of that now, of that object, then the awareness of the object exists. ***Both the objects and the awareness of them exist in parallel. The objects are on the outside and the awareness is within you. However, all of that is one and the same thing, one same phenomenon, it only gets expressed in a different way, outwardly as rough matter, and inwardly as the awareness of it.*** The consciousness and things are one and the same phenomenon, but they are expressed differently because of the varying dimensions in which they coexist simultaneously. Dimensions create difference. The element of air is a thought or an idea in our heads, whereas a thing we hold in our hand is in the element of earth, and it is created by means of intention and energy exertion (the element of fire) and the imagination inspiring us to add the final touch and improve the appearance of the product (the element of water). Existence and consciousness are one and the same, we view existence as rough and outer phenomenon, and consciousness as the fine and inner, although we experience them differently due to the circumstances of physical observation and dimensions of existence.

Everything that is outward is one and the same particle that keeps currently manifesting into various shapes, and the awareness of those shapes is the divine consciousness itself prior to the creation of that particle. That consciousness is in us, that is the consciousness of our soul. It could be said that the divine consciousness stands in the interval between the two vibrations of the "divine particle". Everything vibrates from that one "divine particle", no physical object could exist otherwise but as the conscious intention of the divine consciousness to vibrate in that exact manner, in the form of the chair you sit on, the book, wall, the ground you walk on, the air you breathe... *It would all fall apart into ether if there were no clear conscious intention to exist in such a chosen shape vibrating continuously in a synchronized manner*. The shapes of all the things are actually synchronized vibrations of one "divine particle", that contains all the atoms and molecules. Their synchronization in space and time is a conscious intention. This synchronized conscious intention is the stuff we see, like the chair we sit on, for example. The same works for your body, it is a symbiosis of a multitude of cells (which were bacteria once) that function together in a synchronized way. They are held together by the conscious intention of your soul, its mere presence. When your soul leaves the body, the body will break down into its structural elements. All the events represent the same intention: a synchronized conscious intention. The people you live with, the place and the house you live in, the key events that have redirected your life, all of that is a web of conscious synchronizations. Therefore, it does not do to look at the rough shape in all the things only, objectively speaking no things exist on their own, you can see them primarily as the shapes of consciousness, as living shapes. It is not only that the plants are alive, animals and people too, but that everything is equally alive, only it does not know how to tell you that. It is not only consciousness what you have in your head. Consciousness is everything that exists, and that is the reason why you can have consciousness in your head. Speaking in terms of percentage consciousness occupies far less space in our heads than it does in the overall universe.

It is all one and the same divine consciousness or existence: a physical thing that you are holding in your hand is its furthest and roughest version, and the awareness of it within you is its finest form. All of these phenomena are actually integral parts of yourselves, but divided into the external and rough, and into the inner and subtle existence. Everything you see around you, all the things, love and support you, because everything that exists perceives itself through you, through your consciousness. So, show a little mercy towards everything you see and touch. Your mercy does not have to be only for those you love and for special moments that please you. If we all lived with gratitude and gentleness in our treatment of everyone and everything, our life on this planet would be the same way in response to our original impulse. Animals, too, are grateful for the mercy and tenderness. Let alone life itself! Start off with whatever you are holding in your hand now, and the first person you encounter. Show maximum respect for everything that exists. Do unto others as you would have them do unto you. And never cease with your acts of mercy and respect towards everything, keep them always and everywhere in all circumstances. Mercy and love in this world will never prevail if they get applied only in response to the received mercy and love, as a reaction. We have to create them constantly and provide them despite the fact that we do not receive them, and, especially, where there are none to be found. Only when we create them and provide them by ourselves firstly, we can expect them as a reaction in return. Existence is like a mirror for the consciousness of our soul. The way we are is the way that reflection in the mirror is, and the way our existence becomes. Only when we become the personification of mercy, respect and love, we will begin to receive mercy, respect and love in the mirror of existence, in our immediate surroundings. Even if we do not get it, because of some karmic reasons, at least we will know that mercy and love are at the core of the very existence. When it is conceived once, it is never lost or abandoned, not even during the harshest suffering. A man, who has divine mercy in himself, can only but pity the one who beats him, because he sees the mutual unity with his attacker and all the tragedy of his alienation, that makes him experience suffering and commit acts of violence.

Divine consciousness that vibrates as life energy is the unconditional love that gives us love at any moment, makes our heart beat and our lungs breathe. Strictly scientifically speaking, our body is actually the entire planet Earth, because outside of it, we die immediately. It is sad how unaware we are of the absolute love that keeps us alive every moment of every day. That unconsciousness is the only source of all our suffering. Therefore, our mission in this world is only to reveal and become aware of that universal love.

Therefore, love is not only when you 'make love' with your loved one. Each moment of existence is an act of love, the most intimate moment of two people connecting after a seeming separation from one another. That happens at every moment throughout our entire lives, in everything we observe, communicate and work, at absolutely every moment. During the ecstasy of a love embrace with your significant other, the essence is to know yourself, because the closeness of the soul of your partner brings us closer to the closeness of our own soul. The essence of love regarding the other party is the awareness of him/her, and it depends on our awareness of ourselves. The other person was only the crutch that enabled you to stand up and walk in order to come to yourselves, realizing in the end that you are one. Likewise, the other person perceives himself/herself through your love, if it is the one, if it is real. Understanding is the foundation of true love. In such orgasmic union, a new life is created. It has to be like that, because all the life already rests on that unity, it originates from that unity and is completely dependent on it. That is why love is the fundamental driving life force, the ultimate motive of all work in this world and people's interests.

Similarly, every moment when we touch something, when we only look at some plant (it experiences our look as a touch), when we do anything, the divine consciousness experiences ecstasy because it gets realization of itself through you, the subatomic particles of your hand merge with the particles of the object you touch and the recognition becomes even clearer. That recognition, this state of awareness, is the manifestation of their primordial unity. The primordial unity of everything is the only reality. That is why it is always perfect.

That is why, when the human finally experiences the final awakening, enlightenment or God-realization, they become petrified in awe while looking at their own finger, hand, or the earth, wall, tree, cloud, or even a neighbor who had insulted them before on numerous occasions. All of that disappears, and they is immersed with bliss, in everything the human sees one and only perfect divine consciousness, its presence.

It comes as a great surprise to them, then, because up until this moment, the human has imagined it otherwise or dreamed that all of that was something else, something the external shape makes them to be, while in reality, essentially, it has always been only about the divine unity.

Therefore, in existence itself, there are no changes, it is always as it needs to be. Only our awakening can happen. In the entire universe, that is the only new phenomenon that could happen.

Maybe it is a paradox to say, but let it be said: when the awakening happens, then it is perceived as though it had not happened, at all, that everything in the entire universe was leading to our awakening, that the universe exists because of it, but that its essence is timeless, and in timelessness nothing new can happen. All our illusions, all our dreams and suffering were an integral part of the awakening, part of the perfection. The universe itself is our awakening, our wakefulness, because it has always been our existence. Before awakening, universe was on the outside appearing dead, and after awakening, it reveals itself as our personal living consciousness, our alertness. Therefore, existence and our wakefulness are one and the same. The more awaken we are, the more we see the perfection of that unity.

WHY THE UNMANIFESTED
BECOME MANIFESTED

The divine Absolute does not actually get itself manifested. There is no place to be manifested, because nothing is possible outside of it. It does all of that in its imagination. However, when it comes to the point of imagining something, it is not a fantasy world we are prone to concocting. Its fancy is this entire cosmos and all the life. That is why that imagination looks so real, it has all the properties of reality. The truth is, we are its imagination and we are on the same level with all the other imaginings, and that is why it looks so real to us.

It all happens within because it cannot remain unmanifested. It would be completely abstract then, as nothingness or void. Indeed, its unmanifested essence is emptiness. It cannot sustain itself this way, and as such it comes into paradox with itself. Nothing or the emptiness cannot possibly exist. That is why it must be manifested in the form of its imagination, at least, and with this emanation it strives to express unto itself all its possibilities. It must become something, to avoid the danger of being nothing. For that reason, the divine Absolute manifests itself into the entire cosmos.

We should know that with its manifestation into cosmos, the divine Absolute does not lose anything of itself, it does not change its essence. In other words, cosmos is the divine Absolute itself, its manifested aspect.

On the one hand, the divine Absolute must manifest itself, and on the other hand, nothing can exist outside of it. That is why everything is its imagination, and that is why it is so real.

The very divine Absolute is not aware of itself, because it is so perfectly complete in itself that it does not need any additional awareness of itself. Its sheer existence is the awareness of itself. That is why the essence of consciousness is the very existence, and the essence of existence is the consciousness of oneself. However, because of such nature of consciousness, that is existence, the divine absolute comes to the point of paradox with itself, if it does not manifest all its possibilities. Existence comes in the paradox with itself if it is not aware. The consciousness comes in the paradox with itself if it is not actualized through existence. Therefore, only when it starts manifesting all of its possibilities, the divine Absolute becomes aware of itself. Its manifestation is the act of self-awareness. *Only when the divine Absolute has "lost" itself and manifested into the universe, it began to be conscious of itself. That is why each act of awareness is the act of returning the divine absolute to itself. That is why the consciousness is directly tied with the loss of itself and the returning to itself.*

The manifestation, therefore, takes place for the purpose of self-awareness and all its possibilities. Before it becomes manifested and becomes aware of all its powers and possibilities, the divine Absolute remains the unmanifested void, which is the unsustainability paradox in itself. That is why it needs to get itself manifested, at least within itself and in its imagination, because it has nowhere else to go.

Its manifestation happens as the manifestation of the sum of all of its powers and possibilities. Everything that can be, happens. On the subject of manifestation, this part is the most important for us to understand. ***Absolutely all the possibilities get manifested, everything that is possible in any way, all the oppositions, from the most beautiful and supreme to lowest and the worst.*** The abundance of the manifested phenomena is such that it perplexes us, so we do not see the very nature of manifestation. That is simply everything that is possible, that can be. Nothing else. And that is the essence of existence: it is the field of manifestation of all the possibilities.

The manifestation of everything that is possible implies existence of a variety in space and time, and not uniformity. Therefore, there are places where existence is harmonious, nice and constructive, but also places where it is inharmonious, ugly and destructive. The same applies to time, independently from space, where existence is nicely regulated and harmonious, and other times when it is nothing like that, at all, the times of creation and those of destruction. Therefore, if we find ourselves in chaotic, disharmonious and destructive surroundings and time, we should not think that the entire existence is such. It is such only at this given time and space because it has the freedom to be like that. That freedom is the building block of the perfection of the whole. Were it not for that freedom, the whole as such would not be perfect.

The divine is so grand in its perfection that it can allow for the imperfect parts and diverse time periods on the local scale to take place, in our limited experience. Therefore, even the worst things we can be witnesses to, should not be interpreted as evidence of the imperfection of existence, but only as the imperfection of our perception. Even the worst things are indicators of creativity of perception of the Whole. That is why everything is possible and everything is supported by the whole.

44

The divine Absolute has, with its manifestation, seemingly taken the limitations of our perception in order to experience certain aspects of itself, certain types of experiences. Each part contains and reflects the whole of the divine.

HOW DOES THE UNMANIFESTED
BECOME MANIFESTED

The unmanifested becomes manifested through the different dimensions of existence. We have shown all the dimensions of nature in the picture of pyramidal shape for better understanding. Now, that shape will help us to understand how everything is manifested from one into the myriad. That happens like a prism when light gets dispersed through it creating the color spectrum of the rainbow. All higher dimensions of nature act like a prism, they diffract the consciousness of the divine with its own nature and make it manifest in a different manner, in accordance with each dimension. The consciousness of the divine existence, that is in its essence timeless, looks like it occupies a certain timeframe through the focus of that prism. Complete unity as seen through that prism becomes more and more the world of objects segmented within the category of space and time.

Different dimensions are nothing but different vibrations of the same occurrence, one "divine particle" of the divine Absolute. They start their motion from the sparsest (ether) to the densest (earth, physical world).

Actually, there are dimensions much denser than those of the physical world, but they are unimaginable to us. We do not want to know about them, because to us, they represent everything that is dark and negative. Vibrations of the physical world can be found somewhere in the middle between the densest and the sparsest. The vibrations and influences that we experience as positive, 'heavenly' and 'divine', come from higher dimensions. All vibrations that we experience as negative, "demonic" and "hellish", come from the lower dimensions. We are at the center of a sandwich, placed exactly between them. That is why life here is, at the same time, fun and difficult, on earth there are, side by side, the heavenly bliss and the torture from hell but this is the place where expressing all the oppositions, all the possibilities is the only option. Only under such conditions as these are, the divine consciousness can be crystallized.

Sunlight having passed through the prism becomes variegated, we see all the colors of the rainbow, however, it was the same way before passing. The prism has only made us see it in a different way, we have become aware of the colors this light consists of. Consequently, the prism of manifestation of divine consciousness out of the Absolute neither contributes to nor diminishes anything pertaining to the divine consciousness, it only conditions its manifestation into all of its possibilities. Therefore, the nature of dimensions is such that they only condition all the potential possibilities of the divine to dissolve and manifest, and the divine is always one and the same in everything. The same principle applies here - light before going through the prism is one, white light, and beyond the prism it transforms into all the colors of the rainbow. The prism of dimensions dissolves One into the multitude of all the possible details, into all the possibilities of that One. The divine itself does not undergo any alterations during the process. It always remains the same, what it is – in all its intricacies and possibilities.

Given the tremendous impact the dimensions have on the divine consciousness, the divine consciousness becomes dispersed in all its abilities and is capable of expressing all its possibilities quite concretely once the light of its consciousness reaches the physical 3D plane, which represents the element of earth.

When we put crystal on a colored cloth it then takes on the color of that cloth, even though it merely refracts the color that is not its own. The same happens with the divine consciousness and the consciousness of the soul. Reflecting themselves through different dimensions of existence, they appear to be colored with those dimensions and ways of existence, even though they are essentially independent from any form of existence.

This would be philosophical and somewhat esoteric depiction of how the divine manifests itself into all the phenomena.

This would not be a complete book about the perfection of that manifestation if we did not provide a detailed representation on how everything takes shape.

We have previously stated that the 'divine particle' vibrates out of ether causing the vibrations to become rougher and more complex, until they get manifested into a physical shape, all of which we see in the form of 'matter'. The logical conclusion is that all matter comes from ether.

How does this take place in this three-dimensional universe, in practical terms?

The answer is simple: everywhere and at any given moment.

Ether as a notion existed in all old esoteric schools, up to the beginning of the twentieth century, when Nikola Tesla started to base his inventions on the physics of ether, the inventions that revolutionized and transformed the entire world.[7] At approximately the same

---

7 Information technologies on the whole, as well as telecommunication, are based on three patents by Nikola Tesla from 19th century:

---

time Mendeleyev based his Periodic Table of Elements on ether, as the primary source of all the other elements, but after his sudden and untimely death, it was immediately hidden away from the public eye and changed. The idea of ether was eliminated and today we only know about this shorter and falsified version of the "Periodic Table of Elements". At about that same time, one very suspicious symposium took place where scientists voted ether out of science 11. However, since no proper scientific research is able to come up with a true explanation of anything without ether, terms replacing ether have also been found. The term "black hole" and in recent times "dark matter" should do the job. "Black holes" are, according to contemporary science, huge, dark and scary places in the cosmos, which keep on swallowing time and space, and all the matter, too. Bottomless holes in other words. However, since it dawned on them, over the course of years, that all of it is rather meaningless, someone came up with an idea to attribute some positive characteristics to it, too, and they have in recent times been assigned the job of creating matter.[8]

It was all merely pure ignorance, not knowing the obvious facts that "black holes" are actually the fields of

---

one is the wireless transfer of signal and energy (mobile phones), and the other is four oscillatory circuits in resonance (remote controlling, without which satellites and guiding are virtually impossible), and the third one is AND Logic Gate, a logical circuit in all the computers for the selection of frequencies that enable the triage between the true and the false information (computers). Apart from that, the modern world is set in motion with Tesla's electric motors, lasers and radio signals, and the entire planet earth is illuminated with his light bulbs.

[8] See the book by S. Hawking: Black Holes and Baby Universes. (Black Holes and Baby Universes and Other Essays, by Stephen W. Hawking, Bantam Book, 1993.)

clear space otherwise known as ether. Ether is in esoteric teachings identified as pure space that generates everything else into existence. The name in Sanskrit was *akasha*, which in translation means space. ***Those fields of pure space are actually what we describe here as the interval between two frequencies of the same "divine particle", the interval when the divine consciousness returns to itself.*** Each moment of existence consists of that returning and re-manifestation of the "divine particle". It vibrates in such a way, but never the same, its fine differences in vibrations we can see in fractal geometry and in golden cross-section, and in its widest form in all the laws of nature we have discovered so far.

Those fields of pure space, ether, exist everywhere around us and in everything, in each and every moment. They also constitute everything, and first and foremost, they make up the space itself.

In other words, "black holes" exist everywhere. There are very small ones, and very large black holes. Their size creates the proportions of phenomena and the manifestation of everything.[9] The proportions range from the Absolute which generates timeless space, which, in turn, conditions everything else; followed by all the galaxies; all the stars; our Sun; planetary system around the sun; Earth and all organic world on it; the Moon as the satellite of Earth that represents the proportion of the divine consciousness in the shape of a dream of the human mind or ego, limited by its identification with the body. Each proportion has its number of laws that condition it, the number which progressively grows to an ever lower and lower proportion and greater "distance" from the Ab-

---

[9] On the proportions and the manifestation of cosmos see the book "The Cosmological Lectures" from Peter Ouspensky,

solute, and that means the greater conditionality. The human mind/ego is the most conditioned because it is the farthest point of that manifestation.

Following the set pattern, the biggest "black holes" create galaxies; smaller ones make the stars; even smaller ones create planets, smaller ones than those create conscious living beings, and the tiniest create electrons, which form atoms and all the elements.

Black holes create all of that according to the model of torus.

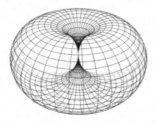

Everything that exists in the physical universe, from electrons to man, stars, and galaxies, exists according to the model of torus.

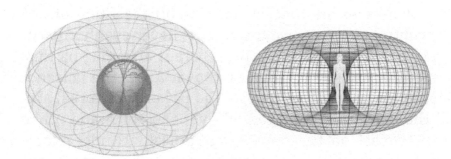

At the center of each torus there is one "black hole", pure space, akasha or ether.

Their different sizes produce all the differences in shapes of everything that exists in the cosmos. The biggest "black holes" create entire galaxies. Smaller ones create stars, but their size is such that, in accordance with their proportion, at the edge of their torus they cause the return field (it arises during interaction with the surrounding space) that creates high vibrations of all the elements, which due to the high vibrations, create high temperature. It becomes manifested in the form of hot plasma we see on the surface of the stars, as their light.

When the "black hole" is smaller, it, again due to the nature of its proportion, on the edge of its torus field, creates hot plasma from all the elements, but it keeps those elements in a cooled off state by its side. That happens because the "black hole" is smaller than the one of the stars and elements can form in a cooler state, not only in the form of plasma, but as concrete elements separate and well-defined in space. That is how on the edges of the smaller "black holes" apart from hot plasma, a cooled crust made up of elements, that we see as planets, is also formed. Therefore, each planet is hollow inside and in its core there is one small star, that has a small "black hole". The planets within their crusts fend off the vibrations of the central sun, because the crust is never evenly cooled. Underneath the cooled surface there is also magma that sometimes erupts as, what is known to us, the volcano. That phenomena, too, follows the patterns of torus, and all the volcanoes scattered all over the earth and other planets exist on the same geographical latitude. Again, not all planets are of the same size, so the bigger ones, with a larger "black hole" in their center have higher temperature, which renders the formation of a hard cooled crust from the elements impossible. Such ones exist in the form of large gas giants (Jupiter, Saturn and Neptune).

When the "black holes" are even smaller, they form the physical bodies of living beings. Then, they are placed in the gravitational center of their bodies. In man, it is about five centimeters (two inches) bellow the navel. That is the famous point *tan tien*, in the system of energetic awareness of the body, *tai chi*. The body derives all the energy for living and action from that point. However, only man can experience the phenomenon of relocating that point, the center of ether, the field of pure divine consciousness. When man sits in the lotus position, in meditation, then the point of the center of torus of his body is lifted up to the area of the heart, to the heart chakra. With arms and legs crossed over, the body is physically and energetically closing itself into the original field of the divine consciousness, with the center of torus placed in the heart. Hence, in meditation man finds his center in the divine consciousness, in *Samadhi*.[10]

---

[10] On the details of practice of meditation see my book "Meditation: First and Last Step. From Understanding to Practice", and about Samadhi in my book "Samadhi: Unity of Consciousness and Existence".

I would not know how to explain all of this any better, with more scientific details, since it is all based on my personal insights which I received after "coming back" from the higher dimensions, from Samadhi, into the physical body.

CONSCIOUSNESS, EXISTENCE
AND THE MAN IN BETWEEN

Consciousness and existence are one and the same, they are only manifested in a different, opposite way.

Consciousness is the finest aspect of existence, existence is the roughest aspect of consciousness.

Consciousness and existence are one and same, organized in such a way that consciousness is of a more subtle structure and can be easily lost, it acts from within and keeps inviting us to become aware of it using our own will, in order to make a conscious effort to always and freely manifest consciousness in existence, to try to exist consciously. Existence is what happens externally, significantly rougher and harder, it keeps hitting us in all possible ways, sometimes as strokes of destiny making us turn toward our inner world, toward the consciousness. The outer world is the type of consciousness that has already objectified and manifested itself in the form of concrete shapes and events. The inner world of the human soul is the consciousness that is of unmanifested nature, where all the potentials of the external manifestations are timelessly condensed.

We are designed in such a way as to enable, through ourselves, their crisscrossing,[11] for them to be recognized as one and manifested as one. To learn to live

---

[11] Hence the symbolism of the cross, resurrection and the metaphor of carrying the cross on one's back.

---

consciously. To realize through a conscious life the divine presence in every moment of reality. It only manifests through an enlightened man in existence. The way it was in one divine whole. It is one, only we do not see it.

Once we reach the finest layer of existence, the quantum field, we observe that it is intangible, that all subatomic particles originate from it, which will upon further complexity become atoms and everything we perceive as the physical world, but also that everything within that universal field is interconnected on the current level, independently from time and space, there is an instant form of communication between everything, that is, it is fully aware of itself. The states of subatomic particles are directly dependent on the presence of the observer, on the conscious subject. Only in the presence of a conscious subject they act as particles, without the conscious observer, they are only a wave of energy, a potential. Therefore, the universal quantum field shows all the quality of a conscious field, the field of consciousness.

All the evidence we have on the quantum field indicate that it is the finest field of conscious existence. The rough world of shapes we are able to perceive with our senses is only the ultimate and the most complex expression of that field of consciousness. Its reverse image. They represent one unique whole. Nothing otherwise could even exist. Everything that you see and perceive, your body, all the beings, all the things around you are only the manifestation of conscious intention wishing to express itself in such a way, in that shape you observe with your senses now. If you view the existing objects as independent material objects, then you are unaware of the true nature of everything that you perceive. As well as of your own true nature. That is the reality an average man in this world lives in.

Why is it so?

Simply because the human body is designed in such a way that it slows down the universal consciousness of existence to such an extent that it only looks like a rough object isolated within space and time. The body is the mechanism that slows down the current consciousness of existence of everything, that displays existence only as rough physical existence, in which separate, independent objects occur in time and space as such.

In accordance with that, the development of human society is designed to slow down the consciousness, to falsely teach us that the consciousness is only material, that matter is unconscious and that everything happens purely by accident or under strict control of the physical laws, meaning the laws that apply *per se* only in the physical world. The development of life is attributed to random evolution.

Science has discovered that the development of one cell, the basic factor of life, is so complex that it is actually perfect, the gene division of a single cell and its growth are so intelligently designed rendering error virtually impossible. Everything performs its task impeccably and all quality product checks exist during the creation of the new DNA. In order to somehow explain the occurrence and the development of life, to hide the role of consciousness playing the key part in progeny, science teaches us today that both life and man originated purely by accident or some mistake throughout the division of DNA, which all happened a long time ago.

Consciousness is not a product of the brain and of the functioning of neurons, the brain is only a receptor of consciousness, the receptor that is designed to slow down the current consciousness of the entire existence to such a slow pace that we experience existence only as the physical phenomena of rough objects isolated in space and time. We view ourselves in much the same way. When that receptor, the brain, becomes damaged and can no longer conduct the consciousness, or when it simply changes its functioning, the man, then, automatically is launched into higher dimensions, out of the body. Observed from the outside, the person becomes unconscious. He actually becomes open for higher dimensions and consciousness of the soul, but if he is firmly identified with the limited consciousness of his body only, he experiences that as if in a dream, relatively foggy and unclear or he fails to remember anything upon the return into the body, if there is no need for him to remember. If it is a mature soul then he can remember everything, it all appears to be a lucid dream, he was aware of the fact he was out of the body.

Memory is not in the brain either, the brain only receives universal consciousness of the quantum field, ether or *akasha*, where all the potentials of existence are situated on one place, everything is already there, everything that has ever happened, is happening or will happen. Here, on the rough plane of existence, only certain possibilities, from that universal field of all the possibilities, become manifested. Memory is only our individual connection with that universal field where everything is located. Upon damaging the brain functions, the connection with that field is lost, which appears like a memory loss to us. That certainly does not mean that memory is in the brain. If the radio is broken, it does not mean that broadcast does not exist.

Actually, there are people with no brains (Dandy Walker syndrome, DWS), who have only a thin layer of cortex of the big brain and emptiness inside, or only water (Hydrocephalus). Those people function in a completely normal way, as students and workers, with high IQ. The percentage of them is very small, and they are considered to be medical phenomena, their identity is often hidden, in order, supposedly, to avoid being discriminated by the society, but it is most likely that they can, with their sheer existence, jeopardize numerous scientific lies about the role of the brain and the nature of consciousness.

Why is body designed to slow down the universal consciousness of existence?

So that the divine consciousness of the Absolute could experience all the possibilities of personal existence, all the details, in all the aspects. It does so via the human body. That is not possible in the realm of impersonal unity in the highest dimension, at the source of all life. The differentiation of the consciousness itself is necessary, firstly into the consciousness and existence, which is the starting point of the "divine particle", and the onward differentiation of existence, initially through all the shapes (minerals), all perception and movement (plants and animals), down to all the events (karma) that express the ultimate reach of events to be made aware of, to know their meaning and purpose. That can only happen in man who has designed the entire nature, as well as himself, in all the dimensions. When the consciousness of existence comes to its own awareness and meaning in man, in other words, when existence is realized as the consciousness itself, the divine, universal consciousness, it is returned to the divine Absolute as its complete awareness of itself. That happens through man and all his experiences.

The human being is designed not only to separate the consciousness from existence, in order to implement all the differentiation of consciousness and existence, but also to reconnect the consciousness of the divine Absolute with existence, actually to discover and actualize their original unison through himself.

The man through whom the original unity of the divine consciousness and existence is actualized is the God-man, the resurrected son of God, the enlightened one, Buddha.

THE NATURE OF MAN

Man is a microcosm, cosmos in miniature, which means that human being is made up of all the dimensions of nature. This conditions the human to think (the element of air); have energy and will, the intention to realize his thoughts (the element of fire); he has imagination with which he explores all the aspects of his ideas, before he materializes them (the element of earth).

However, man is primarily aware of the physical reality only. He is mostly unaware of higher dimensions. He can reside in them only during sleep or during out of the body experiences. That is because of the way the consciousness is organized in man. He is in possession of the lower and the higher consciousness. The organization itself is such because of the nature of human existence and the incarnation cycle.

The structure of consciousness in man is divided into the *physical mind* that is in the body or brain, the *higher mind*, which is beyond the physical body, in the higher mental body, and the *consciousness of the soul* which is above all the bodies of man, above all the dimensions of nature.

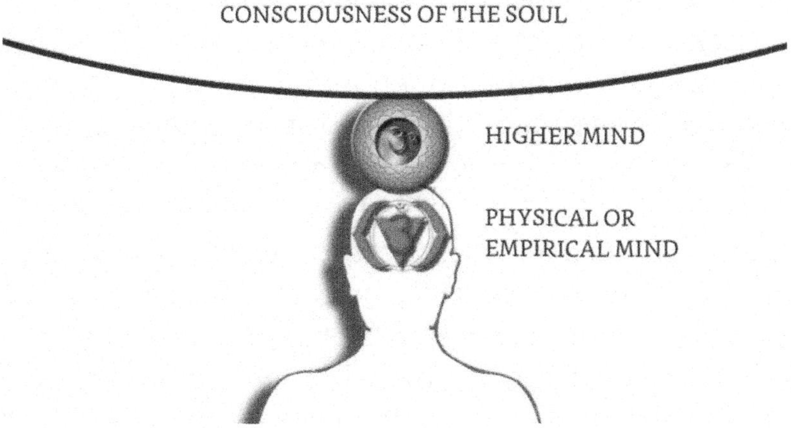
CONSCIOUSNESS OF THE SOUL
HIGHER MIND
PHYSICAL OR
EMPIRICAL MIND

Picture 2

All consciousness in nature and within us stems from the soul, and our souls come from the divine Absolute (God) who generates everything, who generates existence itself. ***Souls are individual emanations or monads of the divine Absolute.***

If that seems abstract, try to understand it in the simplest way possible. The divine consciousness is not only the source of existence, it is existence itself, precisely all of this that is here and now, you and everything around you and inside of you, everything that you see and touch and think at this moment in time. That is that. Nothing is outside of the divine consciousness. Our individual consciousness is the effort to recognize it in all its possibilities, in all the shapes of existence. We come to know it through our individual human dramas and through our common history.

There is a beautiful parable in which the origin of the soul and consciousness is compared to a tree that is put upside down, whose roots are in the sky and branches and leaves on the ground. The common root of the overall existence is in the highest heaven, in the universal quantum field, the finest field of existence, where everything originates as individual phenomenon in space and time. From that in common divine root the individual monads of consciousness branch out similarly to the tree trunk and canopy, which are called archangels and angels in esoteric knowledge, while here, on earth, each conscious being will, in that parable, be one leaf. The individual leaves are individual souls in each man.

Every leaf has its own branch. Only a tree with roots is the source of all souls, or the divine Absolute. The branch which grows out of the basic tree is called the over-soul, it is the source of all other "smaller" souls (smaller branches) that are the source to even "smaller" souls (leaves). In that way, we have ramification from the basic over-soul which is the divine Absolute itself into ever "smaller" souls. However, in all of them the basic over-soul remains present, all the souls are the over-soul that is divided like a broken mirror into tiny fragments, where each of them remains the same, and each soul reflects all the other ones. The divine Absolute splits itself into the more and more self-conscious reflections, otherwise known as individual souls.

The consciousness of over-soul further splits itself in order to finalize the chosen tasks it had desired to experience prior to being born in the body. The tasks can also be divided by their magnitude. There are the major ones, such as creating an entire civilization following the timeline of a certain historic development, either on this planet or some other one. Then, there such tasks like development of a certain nation, family, social organization, religion, up to the personal experiences of individuals who also have a specific set of experiences to go through during the current incarnation.

That is the structure of existence of the divine consciousness, human souls are its manifestations, souls are conscious subjects that perceive the entire existence, and everything exists for the sake of the conscious subjects, in order for them to raise their level of awareness after assorted life experiences. The entire existence is the mirror in which divine consciousness is reflected, the consciousness that has first and foremost been narrowed and individualized in the man.

In our most supreme form we have, as souls, as monads of the divine consciousness, created this entire universe, all the galaxies and stars. That would be the root and tree trunk of the tree in question. With further individualization of consciousness, we created the planets and all organic life. Those would be the branches of the tree. Ultimately, we created all of that in order to be able to express our consciousness individually in one individual being, in this body. Those would be the leaves of our tree of life. An awakened man may well be presented as a flower, and his consciousness as the fruit that contains and reflects the life of the entire tree. In the end, we also created our own oblivion in order to experience this myriad of phenomena. That oblivion is our life on planet Earth.

In order to experience all the individual possibilities, the Absolute has projected this 3D physical world, as his exact opposite. Only in the physical world everything is separate in space and time. In higher dimensions and in the Absolute everything is united in One and that is why it cannot be differentiated. Here, everything is separated for practical reasons, for the purpose of recognizing all the possibilities and details. This world exists because of the differentiation of consciousness. We are conscious subjects that implement that differentiation. We are all leaves on that one, identical, common tree of life.

We are all connected into one, through our higher dimensions. We are only seemingly separated on the physical plane.

Esoteric knowledge teaches us that we have seven bodies, and not only the physical one. We have physical, ethereal (energetic or *pranic*), astral, mental, spiritual, cosmic and nirvana body. All these bodies, besides the physical, belong to higher dimensions. In all of them we reside spontaneously during sleep. Dreams also vary depending on the body in which we find ourselves to be, there are superficial dreams that reflect everyday impressions, and deep dreams that connect us with the higher mind and the consciousness of the soul, as well as with experiences from other incarnations.

The consciousness of the soul does not enter the body directly, and never in its entirety. It is too big and too sublime to reside whole in one body. It is incarnated only partially, in small percentage. Between body and consciousness that is in the body, and that we call here mind/ego, there is a mediator, and that is the higher mind. It is known in other teachings as higher I, or somewhere it is translated as spirit, when spoken about the mind, spirit, soul and the body. The spirit is between the soul and the body. The problem is in different translation of terms so that the meanings of all those terms are mixed and confused from one translation to another. Somewhere it is wrongly assumed that the soul is some psycho-physical mixture of subconscious impressions and energy, and the mind and the higher I are above the soul. That is incorrect.

The correct understanding of the relationship of the consciousness of soul and empirical mind in the body is like in the illustration in this book. The relationship of the consciousness of the mind in the body and higher mind as mediator of the soul can be understood using this little image: mind in the body of a person relates to the one who is at the bottom of the hill, in some labyrinth, who due to his limitations, sees only what is directly in front of him. He sees only what he can see with his senses. At the same time, at the top of the hill there is another person. Both of them are equipped with a radio connection. The one on the top of the hill has a wider view over the vast terrain surrounding the person who is located at the bottom and is going through the labyrinth. The one on the top of the hill can see the entire labyrinth and he can give instructions to the person in the laby- rinth where to go, to warn him of dangers of wrong and harmful turning. Such is the relationship between the consciousness of the mind in the body and the higher mind. It is the same consciousness, only the mind in the body is limited with the body and senses, while the high- er mind is not, it is on the highest dimension, and has a much wider perspective and insight. That is why it is able to lead the lower mind and provide it with the true know- ledge. It does so constantly. However, the lower mind in the body is very limited and it can rarely receive the in- formation directly. The higher mind has to reshape its in- formation, so that they reach the lower mind in the form of visions and inspirations, dreams, and only with their strong impression and attraction they can be recognized as information that came from the higher consciousness, from the soul. Even then, they are misinterpreted as the "voice of God", "angel" or the influence of the "guardian angel". All the cases where man establishes a contact with the divine consciousness happen in such a way, through the higher mind and consciousness of the soul. They have never been communications with God himself. He is not in the business of chatting with people. More precisely, he does not talk to himself.

Those messages from the higher mind are not only dreams and visions, imagination and inspiration. The functioning of the higher mind can also be expressed in a number of ways as physical actions, and all the possible deeds. When the physical mind is so limited or prevented from recognizing the message that came as a result of the vision, dream or in some verbal way, then the consciousness of the soul takes the matters into its own hands by creating events on its own using everything it can, other people, animals, things and situations.

Since for the consciousness of the soul, there is no time, but timeless divine presence, *it is currently incarnated in all the possible incarnations*. Only in consciousness that is limited by the body and mind it looks like it is incarnated over a period of time, in a linear way, firstly in one body, then in another. All our incarnations are simultaneous. That is why we, in all the incarnations, can learn from the experiences that all other incarnations have. Consciousness of all individual incarnations is close-knit and interconnected through an in common over-soul and their exchange of information. That happens through higher dimensions, through dreams. The more we are aware of our higher dimensions, the better connection with consciousness of the soul we have.

Souls have brought many signs to remind them of their original state into this world. Most of these signs and reminders can be found in myths and fairy tales, national dances but also children's games. Hide and seek, for example, is one of the indicators for the souls to remember their original state. In that game, one over-soul is divided into more individual souls. It experiences utter oblivion, then closes its eyes and waits for the others to hide in their bodies and lives. The whole process of awareness – the game – is the process where the over-soul through all the parallel incarnations of individual souls identifies itself, it establishes itself within each individual.

Through our higher dimensions we are connected with all the other souls, and with the entire nature, as well. That connection gives us empathy, the ability of compassion and superior understanding. The ability to love. Love is nothing but our connection with all the other beings, with the whole, through the higher dimensions of our being. The higher we rise in consciousness, and that practically means the more aware we become of higher dimensions, the more we are connected with everything, we experience more in ourselves and us in everything; we are more capable of love and understanding.

Because we have multiple dimensions, we can have out-of-body experiences. If we only had the physical body, we would have the physical mind only, and we would not be able to feel anything toward other people and the whole, we would not have the emotional intelligence and the ability to compare and exchange experiences and information.

Every night, when we sleep, we leave our body and go to higher dimensions, sometimes higher sometimes lower, and most often the first one which is "above" the physical world, and that is astral. Our dreams take place on the astral plane. We can dream only because we have multiple bodies with which we reside in higher dimensions of our own being, and those are, at the same time, higher dimensions of the nature itself. More precisely, we experience those spontaneous exits as dreams just because we are identified with the physical body. Everything outside of it looks fantastic, as if in a dream. When, with the practice of meditation, we become aware of those higher dimensions of our being, then we can enter them consciously, and abandon the physical body with full awareness in order to move through space and time. When we do this consciously, we begin to receive information from the consciousness of the soul in a much better way.

When the connection with the higher mind becomes stronger, through out-of-body experiences, then at the same time our ability to love everything, all the beings, becomes much stronger, and together with love, we also learn to develop the ability to understand our fellow human being. All of that is connected: our overcoming of the identification with the body and mind, connecting with higher mind and consciousness of the soul, the ability to understand and love everything that exists in any way possible. All of that is one and the same thing.

By making ourselves aware of the higher dimensions of nature and our own being, we connect with everything else, because those higher dimensions are not outside of us, they are our deeper nature, what is the most intimate to us.

THE NATURE OF HUMAN SOUL IS A TESTIMONY ON ALL THE POSSIBILITIES OF THE DIVINE CONSCIOUSNESS

When we said that the essence of existence is for all the possibilities of the divine consciousness to be able to manifest, that meant two things.

Firstly, that means *absolutely all the possibilities*, because it is about the potentials of the Absolute. Everything-that-is is manifested as everything-that-can-be. Everything means absolutely everything, both good and evil, in all variants. That implies complete freedom for all the possibilities. That is why freedom is a double-edged sword, it gives us possibilities and both positive and negative changes and states. It is very wrong to connect the term freedom with something pertaining to positive only. There is freedom to experience the negative, as well. The divine consciousness is a precondition for everything, it gives the freedom of manifestation to everything, to the most negative possible things and phenomena also. We have the freedom to be negative, to trap ourselves in all the possible negative states. Not only to set ourselves free and be good. That means that the divine consciousness is a precondition for all of that and supports it as one of its options. That is why the basis of everything is positive, life itself is a positive phenomenon, although negative things could also happen. We experience things as negative only to the degree we are unaware of the true nature of life. We see everything as good when we base our life on the support of the divine consciousness.

In fact, we have trapped ourselves here when we incarnated, away from much greater consciousness of our soul, which we had had before birth, we limited ourselves to this physical body and world, in order to experience what we originally intended. All of that was made possible by the absolute freedom of the divine consciousness to experience all the possible states and aspects. That freedom is actually the divine love. It facilitates and supports everything. Even the misconception that we are separated from the divine, that we are in suffering. And that is the freedom we have, when we are supported by the divine love. All the time, we are in the divine, because we can never be outside of it, and we imagine that we are outside of it, that something is missing, that things are wrong and imperfect. The fact that we can be in such a state is evidence of the absolute freedom that conditions everything, and not that we are truly outside of the divine. Only the divine generates the illusion that we are outside of the divine. That is the ultimate freedom that it provides. That is the ultimate creativity in manifestation of the divine. That is the evidence that the divine love always exists as the basis of everything. It supports us in everything. That is why we can be equally successful in everything, both in good and constructive actions as well as in bad and destructive ones. The entire life was given to us as perfect, but if we do not see it and respect it in our freedom and illusion, if we threaten it, that is not the mistake of the perfection of divine consciousness, but only of one piece of it that due to that perfection, has the ability to do whatever it wants. That small piece is us, human beings. And only because of that freedom to experience wrong, we come to the awareness of what is right.

The testimony about all the possibilities encompasses the entire spectrum of all the possibilities, from the extremely positive ones to those extremely negative. Sports games show the positive manner in which the consciousness of the soul experiences all of its states and possibilities in this world, in the physical body. People are the most beautiful and the happiest when they experience their ultimate abilities in sport. For that reason, sport is so attractive for people. Actually, there are testimonies of memories souls had before birth that they, in heaven, also have sports competitions.

Sport, work and creative endeavor are ways in which consciousness of the soul manifests its values. Wars are experiences of the exact opposite option, when people experience all of their flaws and drawbacks of the mind, separations from the consciousness of the soul, in a negative and much harder way. However, using both ways, they bring themselves closer to the consciousness of the soul.

Actually, man is drawing nearer to the consciousness of the soul every moment of every day in all ways possible, he always experiences divine consciousness, he lives in it and off it, it is only a question of the maturity of his individual mind how he experiences that subjectively. If he understands and accepts, then he experiences his existence through positive and creative experiences, if he closes himself off (ego) and therefore resists and negates life, he then goes through many negative and destructive experiences. It is not a form of punishment, at all. That is a spontaneous reaction, a mirror reflection. Nature is the mirror in which the human mind becomes reflected, it is the conscious subject of the objective nature. The mirror bears no responsibility on the kind of reflection it produces.

If you think you did not have a loving parent, if you feel lonely now, you are mistaken. You have had and you always have the best parent, the divine love that all else is predicated upon. It gave you each breath and each heartbeat, every joy of cognition you have ever had. And all the misconceptions and suffering it has allowed you to experience in order to be able to experience the joy of repentance and awakening.

The entire process of human incarnations is a process of growing in individual awareness of the presence of the divine love that precedes everything; the entire development of human civilizations is the development of collective awareness of the divine love that precedes everything. If awareness of the divine presence in this limited dimension full of illusions has not been realized completely yet because of our limited perception, that does not mean it does not exist and that, in the long run, it will not be realized here, right here on planet Earth.

There must be a conscious subject who all those possibilities will be manifested to, in order for them to be made conscious and that consciousness to return to the divine Absolute through itself. The conscious subjects of existence are individual consciousnesses or souls. Those are to varying degrees all conscious beings in the universe. The most conscious beings are human beings, us. The final knowing and return to divine consciousness happens in us.

Therefore, when some possibility of existence happens, and the conscious subject experiences it, he becomes aware of it, and automatically the divine Absolute becomes aware of it, too, because all conscious beings are connected with it, all of them are a small reflection of the divine consciousness, according to the model of hologram and through ramifications of over-soul into the smaller and finer individualities.

When we perceive and experience something, it is then brought back through the consciousness of our soul to the divine Absolute.

Everything happens for the purpose of being perceived and experienced, realized, and returned as the awareness of the phenomena to the divine Absolute. That is the only purpose of all the possible events in universe. After all, we have said that universe itself exists with the aim that the divine becomes aware of itself.

Our soul is the witness of all the happenings, of everything that takes place. *Everything happens because of our souls*, because of the divine consciousness. The nature is the field of manifestation of everything that is possible to manifest, whereas our souls are transcendental, independent witnesses of all the events, and the awareness of all the happenings returns to the divine source. *The souls themselves do nothing*, because in the essence of their existence is the Absolute who is already everything. That is why souls are only witnesses. They are the very presence of the divine consciousness in existence. The physical body forms around them firstly, then the environment in which that body will function while gathering and perceiving all the possible experiences. In order for those experiences to avoid being chaotic, for the order and meaning to be established easier, the experiences of our incarnations are grouped together according to their themes, although there is a good part left for the manifestation of free will and coincidences. If everything is already determined by destiny, there would be no place for the creativity of consciousness, and creativity is essential in conceiving the perfection of everything.

That is why nothing ever repeats itself in universe. Everything is unique because at the moment when the conscious is perceived, by some conscious being, witness, human or non-human, the consciousness of that is fulfilled and returned to the divine. That does not have to go on happening any more, the happening further develops and takes on new shape. That principle works for absolutely everything that happens, for everything you have ever done in your life, for all you have ever seen, for each phenomenon around you that has ever taken place in the entire world.

Only there, where conscious subjects are nowhere to be found, existence is inert and without change, that is, the changes take place albeit very slowly following their own inertia, with the involvement of the accidental external, mechanical influences. Those are the places which we see as deserts, lifeless planets.

The higher number of conscious subjects and the more the time speeds up and, the changes grow faster and faster in pace. Not only time, but space also adapts to the speed of time and the type of experiences that begin to take place. The experiences become finer and finer. We view that subtleness of experiences and acceleration as the development of culture and civilization. The dawning of civilization starts from the simple and primitive experiences and grows to be more complex and refined. That is why civilizations can be found only where there are conscious subjects, and each civilization is as successful and advanced as the subjects that make it are more aware.

The moment the consciousness of phenomena makes a way back through our soul to the divine whole, it is experienced as love toward the whole and by the whole. Divine love is the awareness of the divine of itself in us. Divine love is no different than existence itself, or the consciousness itself.

SCIENTIFIC EVIDENCE
OF EXISTENCE OF PERFECTION

It could be said that practically all the scientific discoveries reveal the perfection of existence, the perfect creativity of consciousness. In order to see existence as perfect, we only need to arrive at a more thorough understanding of what it truly is. Science helps us with that. Not always. Interpretations of scientific discoveries are something completely different, often reverse of the truth, in public presentations of scientific discoveries, politics still plays the key role. Such politics is based on concealing existence of higher dimensions and dealing exclusively with the physical world, the so-called "matter", the one we can perceive with our senses and only things which can be physically measured. That is justified because it is based on elementary principles of scientific research, but it is restricting for the comprehensive perception of reality. It already exists the way it does, it influences us with all of its higher dimensions, it cannot wait for the scientific research of human society on this planet to develop well enough for us to be able to work with extrasensory dimensions of existence.

The discoveries themselves point to the divine consciousness being at the base of everything, as well as the crucial position of man in the entire order of reality.

We will remind ourselves of the three most important discoveries for our story.

The first one is quantum physics and the discovery of the role of the observer in the experiment.

Quantum is essentially the energy phenomenon, it consists of energy vibrations, which, amongst everything else, can acquire the type of quality to manifest in the form of material phenomenon. However, whether the quantum will manifest itself as a wave or as a particle, does not depend only on the interpretation of the observer, but also on the presence of the observer and its intention as to how the quantum will manifest itself. When the observer, a man, is present in the experiment with the intention to prove that quantum energy is a particle, such result follows suit, quantum energy starts behaving as a particle, and when the experiment is set to prove that quantum energy is a wave, once again, we achieve the corresponding result. Conscious intention determines the result. All of this reveals something that is even deeper than physical phenomena, even deeper than electromagnetic power, it reveals the consciousness itself. It has been discovered that behind the electromagnetic power of the quantum field consciousness exists that manages everything, the entire nature, and the consciousness in question is also the consciousness of the observer, the man, the subject in this experiment. It has been discovered that consciousness is the essential factor in the phenomenon of nature.

The conscious connection between subatomic particles has also been proven in the experiments connected with EPR paradox (Einstein, Rosen, Polanski) in which one subatomic particle is divided in two, entwined with one another in a quantum manner. As soon as one property is measured (its physical size) against one such occurring particle, the same property of the other particle would receive a complementary (opposite) value immediately (Aspect, 1980). Although particles themselves were very far apart, they behaved as though one particle instantly becomes aware of the property of the other one. This is called a paradox because it appeared that information between the two particles travels at the speed much higher than that of the speed of light, which is considered to be impossible. This phenomenon is explained with existence of quantum field that is non-local, that is, identical at every single point of time and space, as if each point of universe contains within itself all the information of the whole universe. That is called non-local communication of the quantum field.

The same was done with human DNA; the DNA of one person was divided and parts were scattered all round, when one part was stimulated, instantly that influence was felt on the other distant part. They reacted as if they were still together, even though they were not. All of this showed that the phenomena of telepathic perception and numerous "occult phenomena" could easily be explained with the nature of the quantum field.

The second one is a cosmological theory of the Strong Anthropic Principle (SAP) according to which the visible properties of the universe, the way they are in everything, are not a product of coincidence or natural selection among the numerous possibilities, but they are rather a consequence of a completely specific purpose: the creation of conditions for the origin of the conscious subject. That principle says: "Universe must have such properties which allow for the development of life at a certain stage of its existence". This is further continued with the explanation that the universe is created with the aim of occurrence and sustainability of the observer, and observers are necessary for existence of universe. This complements the first discovery on the deciding role of the conscious subject in the fundamental happenings of nature.

The third scientific evidence of the perfection of everything provides us with the data achieved upon the measurement of background radiation (satellite Planck, 2013), which proved conclusively that universe is a hologram, because observed from the Earth, it looks like Earth is at the center of cosmos. When results from the satellite are depicted in the form of 3D sphere, a ball is obtained, that clearly shows that it is divided by a line in the middle of the two halves. The entire sphere of cosmos is divided with the line of delimitation into two halves. Actually, the measurements of the background radiation (the farthest radiation on the verge of cosmos) have shown that the entire universe exists according to the model of torus in the same way like the earth does, that it has equatorial area in the middle of its sphere, which is aligned with the Earth's ecliptic and equinox (which astrophysicists named the "Axis of Evil" – maybe because those results threaten to ruin all their current fabrications about the nature of reality they have made their careers on). If we observed the ultimate boundaries of cosmos as the sides of a huge ball viewed from its center, and projected the ecliptic observed from the Earth (the center of the ball) all the way to the boundaries of that ball, meaning universe, it would match perfectly with the equatorial line of the cosmos, with the "Axis of Evil". It is established that all background radiation goes towards the Earth, from all sides. All of that proves that we are in the center of cosmos, and that again proves the key role of the observer or a conscious subject. But that does not prove, however, that any real center exists and that we are in it. That is why the universe is a hologram, every observer from any other corner of the universe can see the same image of cosmos as we do from the Earth. Because of the holographic nature of the universe, each point of observation is identical to all the other points of the holographic whole, there is no up and down, left and right, center and periphery, large and small. There is only the perfect unity of everything.

These recent measurements have definitely confirmed the earlier theories of the Strong Anthropic Principle and holographic universe and bound them together in one whole.

In addition to this, as an illustration for the consciousness being at the base of emergent reality, we can further add the story of the Sun and the stars. The activities of the sun are carefully monitored and it was proved that they have had a crucial influence on geological and climate changes throughout the history, and together with all of these attributing factors, they have largely influenced the development of human civilization. Scientists observing the sun have recently come to the conclusion based on statistical activity of the sun, that its activities are seldom uniform, that there is a pattern of solar activities which depends on the movement of the Earth. Namely, for the last 8,000 years, sun has been relatively stable, the last stronger activity hitting the Earth took place in 1859. without causing major havoc since it affected the few telegraphic cables which were in existence back then[12]. If a solar activity of this magnitude were to happen today, it would destroy all the existing electronics on Earth which would set us back to the Middle Ages. It is a known fact that from the middle of the twentieth century, when the development of electronics soared rapidly, the sun avoids aiming its bigger eruptions of solar winds

---

[12] The event was called the "Carrington event" named by the British astronomer Richard Carrington who observed a solar flare preceding a geomagnetic storm.

in the direction of the Earth, to the point that the sheer number of them has seriously decreased. Much like when someone is about to sneeze so he moves his head to the other side to avoid exposing you. It is noticeable because there have been powerful eruptions of the solar activities, much stronger that the one in 1859, but not in the direction of the Earth, one such example was in July 2012. If any of them hit the Earth, that would have a major influence on the way of life and civilization as we know it. Since the Sun, at the same time, rotates on its axis and Earth revolves around the Sun, the probability of such a thing happening by chance equals zero. It is perfectly clear that someone controls that roulette consciously. All of that leads to the conclusion that the Sun behaves in a conscious manner like a guardian to the Earth, it avoids endangering it with any kind of eruptions, solar flares, coronal explosions, geomagnetic storms.[13]

The behavior of all the stars contributes additionally to that conclusion. They, namely, do not even comply with Newton's laws of gravity in their movement across galaxy. According to those laws bodies closest to the center of the galaxy would have to move faster than the ones near the outer edges. In reality, it is opposite. The ones at the edges of galaxy move faster than those in the close proximity to the center. As if all of them are placed on some invisible wheel that keeps moving them in a synchronized way. In order to somehow explain the invisible connection of stars, scientists have come up with one more phrase for deceiving the public, "dark matter". In reality, this is used to avoid recognizing that everything works in accordance with the quantum physics of ether,

---

[13] On the conscious behavior of the Sun see the work of Dr. sc. Robert M. Schoch.

the quantum field, which is essentially electromagnetic, that all cosmic forces are electromagnetic forces, gravity included, that everything is energy and that energy behaves in a conscious manner.

All scientific research, strictly speaking, prove the theory of intelligent design which suggests that nature and life rely on some higher consciousness, rather than some material causes and circumstances, that consciousness does not originate from matter, but the other way around, that what we wrongly call "matter" (quantum physics has proven that it does not exist) all stem from consciousness, from the intelligent design. Science proves that there is no way that DNA could have occurred by evolution in any way possible, but only through an intelligent design[14]. One of the obvious proofs is in the following. All life rests on the division of DNA, whereas DNA division cannot take place of its own accord, that complex task is performed by proteins. However, the code for the formation of proteins is placed within the DNA itself. So, who is older, the chicken or the egg? It is obvious that both had to be formed at the same time, designed by some higher consciousness.

It is similar with the stars. For them to be created heavy elements are needed, which originate from the stars themselves, with their decomposition. Both stars and their elements had to be created together, designed by some higher force.

All relevant scientific evidence proves that evolution does not exist and that the entire life is created by

---

[14] You can receive more information on this in the work of Stephen Meyer: Signature in the Cell: DNA and the Evidence for Intelligent Design, as well in the work of Nobel laureate Francis Crick who discovered DNA: Life Itself: Its Origin and Nature.

higher intelligence. There is no valid evidence to support the evolution of Darwin's type. There is only adjustment to the living conditions of the environment. The way of reproduction and nutrition of many animal species would not be possible if they evolved gradually over time. Their being had to be created all at once, designed in its entirety, and not developing in stages. The point of everything is that higher consciousness that created life is what has always been called divine consciousness, God, or consciousness of our soul.

The planet Earth is in the same way consciously designed and organized. Its shape, distance from the sun and movement are perfectly consciously designed so they enable organic life on the surface of this planet. It is impossible for such movement and rotation with oscillations that illuminates both hemispheres equally, the northern and the southern one, to occur spontaneously. Satellite measurements concerning the age of the bottom of the sea prove that the earth actually grows, it is blown up like a balloon as compared to before when it was much smaller. There was much more dry land mass in those days, with the expansion of the Earth, plates broke away from one another and spread. Today, even with all the evidence, the false theory of Pangaea prevails, and we are still taught that the earth's crust (tectonic plates), mysteriously glides on the flaming core.[15]

---

[15] The theory of the expanding Earth originated back in 1889 and 1909 when Roberto Mantovani published his theory on the expanding Earth and the movement of continents. The theory was further upgraded with the model presented by an Australian geologist Warren Carrey in 1960s. On the possibilities of a growing Earth, geologists like: Vedant Shehu, James Maxlow, Stavros Tassos and others, contemplated while researching the land mass matching on both the Pacific and the Atlantic coasts, the geological implications of the sur-

All organic life on this planet is directly dependent on humus, a thin layer of soil that is organized with the type of intelligence that can only equal the one that organized the DNA and cells. Humus is created with the symbiosis of plants, bacteria and animals well-coordinated into a perfectly functional system. That symbiosis is not possible without a conscious intention. The ground we walk on being completely unaware of our actions, is alive and conscious, in the same way plants and animals are.

All of that is scientifically proven, but consciousness (intelligent design) is still denied access to the world of science.

Everything we have previously stated represents scientific evidence for our topic, proving that existence is perfect, which further means that the whole is conscious, and as such, it is a perfectly positive phenomenon.

However, we cannot use all scientific evidence for our topic of perfection, because science as we know it today, does not include all the dimensions, but only the material ones, either sensory or empirical. That is justified, because science must be based only on what is measurable and experimentally provable. Science deals with the physical laws only, but the physical world is not the only one that exists, it is actually the last one that exists, it is only the base on which all higher worlds are projected, all the higher dimensions.

Apart from the higher dimensions being hidden from the public, the truth of human soul is also hidden away from people. In science, it is either negated or the

---

face curvature measurements and searching for the causes of, in modern-day terms, impossible size of the dinosaurs and other animals, plants and bugs in the conditions of the Earth's smaller gravitational pull. Nikola Tesla also spoke of the Earth, all planets and the entire cosmos growing as a result of Ether.

term of soul is reduced to some unclear concoction of life energy, mixed with psyche and its impression. That confusion is spread to the world through yet another branch of science called psychology. Before scientific development, the same truth of the soul was hidden in religions. There, it was mystified and projected into divine spheres out of reach of common folk, and before any attempt at comprehending its functioning, church as an institution was placed in the form of a barrier. If the church does not grant so, you cannot save your soul. Not so long ago, it openly charged for the salvation of the soul. It does the same today, but this time - secretly.

The essence of this problem is that the theory of ether is not permitted in science, because in esoteric science which encompasses all higher dimensions, ether is the highest and the most subtle dimension, it corresponds to consciousness. If everything is based on consciousness, then other paradigms which are based on scientific mirage and religious stories for young children, would not find place in the life of modern people. It looks like people are not sufficiently mature to take their responsibility as conscious beings. That is why this world looks imperfect.

Apart from the experimental physics, both spiritual science and philosophy confirm our standpoint on the perfection of existence. The oldest spiritual writings in this world clearly state the same: Tao Te Ching, the Upanishads, Vedanta, esoteric schools of both the East and the West, Hermeticism, Plato's philosophy is completely dedicated to this subject, as well as his heritage, Plotin, Baruch de Spinoza, Jacob Böhme, Meister Eckhart speak of our subject, and especially Friedrich Wilhelm Joseph von Schelling in the works Philosophy and Religion (Philosophie und Religion, 1804), and 'Of the I as the

Principle of Philosophy' (Vom Ich als Prinzip der Philosophie, 1795),' Philosophical Investigations into the Essence of Human Freedom' (Philosophische Untersuchun-
gen über das Wesen der menschlichen Freiheit, 1809) and
'About the World soul' (Von der Weltseele, 1798), using
good, old, philosophical terminology he presents a great
number of his ideas that correlate to the ones we present
here. After Schelling, only Bhagavan Sri Ramana Maharshi clearly spoke about the unity of the Absolute and our
soul, of the perfection of existence, actually, he testified
to that much more with his personal example and presence, than his speech.

After Schelling, the reign of materialistic science
began, and with it, the industrial revolution, that not only
materialized and mechanized human life, but also his
mind and view of the world. People distanced themselves
from the subject of eternity, the relationship between the
Absolute and their own soul, from their perfect unity.

THE PERFECT SUMMARY OF THE FIRST PART

We have examined all the basic reasons of why existence is perfect and why we do not see it as such. We have primarily ascertained that the entire existence is only one unique whole, which we have named the divine Absolute, that keeps manifesting itself as its own opposite quality, projecting itself into a multitude of shapes and phenomena in accordance with the model of hologram, and that means, it always remains one and the same interconnected whole, even though it becomes expressed in the form of a multitude. Each piece reflects the whole. The manifestation of the Absolute takes place across several dimensions. In each dimension existence becomes rougher and more complex, so the one that resides in the lower and rougher dimensions can only be less and less aware of what can be found in the higher and finer ones. That is why we do not perceive the entire reality as the perfect whole, because we perceive existence with our own limitations, viewed only from the lowest and roughest dimension, from the physical world of rough objects, limited with the body that is designed to slow down the current happenings of the consciousness.

Existence is one unique perfect whole and everything that exists acts as the proof for this, only when we take a closer look and understand it more carefully. For example, perfection is the most clearly reflected in the appearance of beauty and harmony. The experience of beauty would not exist if perfection did not exist at the base of that experience. The beauty of nature brings people closer to the experience of perfection of existence in the easiest and the best way. The experience of beauty is actually only our emotional response to experiencing the perfection of existence since our mind is incapable of it. Emotions can perceive deeper than the mind can, and while the mind only uses physical senses, emotions can go to higher dimensions and transmit information the mind could never extract from there. The mind is only bound to the physical body and to its individual contents, emotions are connected to astral body which overcomes the physical body, and that is why emotions are open to all the impressions. We also have a higher mind of our mental body and intuition. Mind receives all the information from the higher bodies and dimensions, but it cannot move in them. If it could, it would be lost in them. The limitations of the mind in the body have the role of safety fuse and control, stability and coherence.

We are attracted by everything that is beautiful, we search for the beauty in everything and we always aspire to it, because beauty is the expression of perfection which is at the base of very existence. It is not only aesthetic beauty we have in mind here, but the beauty of a moment, the perfection of that moment. In people beauty comes from their personality and action, the ability of understanding, that is what makes people beautiful and attractive, not the beauty of the face that can also be deceiving.

The same works for love. Love is only an emotional experience of the unity of the overall existence, and there could be no unity if existence were not perfect and complete in itself. We all strive toward that unity, toward the experience of love in all ways possible. Even in the ways which are impossible. That aspiration is so strong and ingrained that we try to achieve it in the wrong ways, as well. However, since we claim here that everything is perfect, we also have to stress that imperfect aspiration toward love, of the type that can be found in some violent acts, it is only an indirect way to come to the awareness of the right way of knowing love and perfection. Every bully and sinner must face the consequences of their misdeeds in order to repent. The repentance itself is possible only because we are faced with the perfection of existence.

It could be said that the only reason why we make mistakes, is to be convinced of the perfection of the divine consciousness and its omnipresence. That is the reason why sin is so appealing. Only the sinner can become a saint. Our body and our lives are actually designed so that we do not experience anything directly, but it can be done only indirectly, gradually, piece by piece, for us to examine and become aware of all the possibilities, and the probing is manifested as mistakes. Due to our sensory limitation, we see the least what is the most obvious, what is before our eyes, the very nature of reality. We have to come to everything in a harder way, indirectly, through experiencing all the possibilities. That is why we are here. That is why we are designed the way we are, not to be able to become aware of the reality all at once and directly, but indirectly, through all the conceivable and inconceivable experiences.

The perfection of existence is expressed in an indirect manner in this dimension, which is very low and conditioned. It is very rarely expressed in a direct way, because:

- it passes through different dimensions;
- because it has several causes in accordance with circumstances; and

- because there are more conscious subjects, in order to make existence conscious and to be experienced in all possible ways.

Those are simply the conditions of contemporary existence we are in on this planet earth. Because of all of that, we should not label anything as sinful or wrong. We only need to understand the world we live in, the nature of reality.

Perfection is reflected in the presence of love and beauty. The more the love and beauty are present, the more the perfection becomes expressed. The more people in their illusions grow distant from the perfection of existence, from the life itself, the less love and beauty is abundant in this world. The good and enlightened man is always attractive to us, pleasant, dear and somehow beautiful, no matter what he looks like. People who are narrow-minded, negative and destructive are always surrounded by ugly and rough phenomena. We always feel repulsion towards them. Unless we are on the similar wavelength vibration with them. Similar attracts similar, and prefer to co-exist as such.

The perfection of existence as the source of meaning and harmony is the source of all spirituality, the inspiration to all the poets, the chief goal of all the philosophical systems and religions. All descriptions of the higher, divine worlds and phenomena are the descriptions of the perfection and indescribable beauty.

The perfection of existence is what attracts us to the beauty of nature, what rejuvenates and heals us, that is why we feel that fruits of nature feed and heal us. All the beauty and harmony in nature we are able to perceive is the reflection of perception that the entire universe is perfect and exactly the way it should be at any given moment. Every cat that sleeps in the sun knows that.

Man, on the other hand, because of the slowed-down consciousness in the body, needs much more to recognize the same. He needs to pass through all the drama of life, of dying and being born. But that drama is also perfect at every moment, much like everything else, because everything happens within the divine consciousness, never outside of it. It is not possible otherwise.

Goodness points in direction of perfection which is the foundation for all existence, even more so than beauty alone. Goodness and mercy are nothing but conscious actions harmonized with the perfection of existence. Acting in accordance with reality is right and proper, expressing the goodness of our heart is the highest achievement. That is why it brings us positive vibrations and good mood, favorable consequences, too; it always shows itself as the right, the perfect one. Negative conduct always brings the reverse: negative vibrations and moods, negative consequences, too, because it is in conflict with reality. Good and evil are merely harmonious or disharmonious compatibility with reality, nothing else. Everything that is good is the picture of harmony, all that is evil is at odds with reality, resisting reality, insisting on one's illusion that reality is something else, and not what it actually is.

The disharmony itself can exist because of the perfection of existence itself. It would not be able to be perfect if it did not have the ability to enable everything into existence, and the possibility to experience its own opposition (the ugly, the evil and wrongdoing), as well.

However, it is difficult to tell the difference between the good and evil, right from wrong, harmonization with the reality and disharmonization, for the same reason we fail to perceive the whole of reality, since it is multidimensional and our perception is limited. Likewise, the subject of our life experiences is such that it has to contain the awareness of the wrongdoings, in order to become aware of the right ones. There are also subjects of karmic tasks that cannot be accomplished within the duration of one incarnation only, which take multiple reincarnations to be sorted out. Therefore, do not be surprised if you do not understand anything that happened to you in this, one life. You do not know the entire story, you did not watch the entire series of all incarnations needed to understand the whole story. If you are a failure and loser in one episode, or one life, it does not mean that you will be that by the end of the show, when you finally realize who you are. (I spoil the ending for you now: at the end you always win, you realize that you are the divine whole that becomes aware of itself through all the experiences of existence).

The final conclusion of this introductory part is plain and obvious: if we do not see something, it does not mean it does not exist. If we do not see existence as perfect, it does not mean it is not as such. Even if we in our current circumstances experience something negative and destructive, it does not mean that existence is like that in its entirety and its essence. On the contrary, it only shows and proves how much existence is comprehensive and perfect, when absolutely anything is possible in it.

Life and existence are such that they cannot be comprehended by what the senses can perceive and what the mind can grasp. There is more than meets the eye in that area. The very size and complexity of the world and existence, from the subatomic world through the life of cells and nature of events in life drama, are such that everything points to a much wider context than what we perceive with our senses and understand with the mind.

The nature is perfectly economical and logical. It does not go about creating anything unnecessary and wrong, therefore, it would not create this vast universe, so perfectly composed only to have its prize possession, the most perfect, human beings, do nothing but be born, nourished, reproduced and eventually died. The complexity of life clearly shows that there has to exist much more than what is superficially visible. The nature of the world in which we live proves that it is much wider and more complex than our perception can absorb. We can see the most obvious proof for this in people. Human characteristics that create the drama of life are such that they cannot be explained with material causes that originate from the life itself, nor the influences of the environment in which a person lives. There are huge differences among people and differences in character and intelligence that cannot be explained with material causes within the span of one life. All facts lead to the conclusion that there are causes that overcome the birth and the death of one body, the wider context and causality that overcomes one life.

That is also evident when people sacrifice themselves for ideals. Big portion of human life is actually some form of a sacrifice, dedication to someone or something. Actually, life devoted to self-indulgence is inferior and often destructive. The very act of sacrificing oneself for some cause is based on the cognition that there is something higher than the body and mind, recognizing the consciousness of the soul, directly or indirectly, regarding some ideal or life of our beloved one. Every type of self-sacrifice is an act of the transcendence of the mind and body in favor of higher consciousness or certain principles. To what a degree this higher principle is more important than the body and mind, can best be seen in the fact that sacrificing is often followed by ecstasy and absolute conviction.

There is simply no economical justification for the creation of such huge and complex existence and life, if the life of one being is only reduced to the conception, birth and dying, if that is everything that happens, if there is nothing outside of it, before and after. If the basis of cosmic constants were only a little different, the conscious life would not exist, and according to that, all cosmos exists exactly as it is, for the origin of conscious beings. All that effort and creativity would be meaningless if the life of a being were reduced to mere physical survival. All life shows us at every moment and in everything that it is perfect, and that it goes far beyond our perception.

If we were able to see the fundamental constants the entire cosmos rests on, we would see that cosmos would not exist if it were not exactly like this, the way it is at this moment, in everything, in each, even the tiniest detail. If you were not reading these lines right now, if you were not located exactly there where you are, in such an environment and life situation that you find yourself in at the moment, and if every thing you can see right now were not where it is - *this entire cosmos would not exist*. Such is the nature of the perfection of existence. *It cannot be any different than it is at every given moment.*

PART TWO

THE PERFECTION OF DYING AND BEING BORN

Having displayed the nature of reality and why it is perfect, we will display this perfection in our life experience.

The first and the most universal experience we have is linked to dying and being born. It is often a focal point for all the misunderstandings that may arise.

Nothing scares us more than death itself. The reason for this lies in the fact that we do not understand the nature of birth, what actually took place when we were born. Additionally, why we were born in the first place.

Based on what we have already seen on the true nature of reality and existence itself, it may only become clearer to us that we are never detached from any of it, it is not possible. Therefore, the same thing that applies for us, applies for the nature of the absolute existence, the divine consciousness.

The essence of existence is that it always exists, timelessly. Non-existence is not an option. Everything we have ever experienced, thought, said or done, all our memories are a part of the divine whole, a contribution to the possibilities of the divine whole, and none of that can disappear. Ever. None of it was brought about into existence, there is no point of origin, it is only us doing it to ourselves, we have expressed our experience through ourselves and all the available potentials from the covert into the overt, to the manifested state. No thought is ever new, no word or deed, either. Only their potentials for emanation, their combinations may be new.

The same works for our essence, as well. We exist timelessly, forever. We never appeared and we will never disappear, either. We were never born nor shall we die. The show of being born and dying is merely a performance of the consciousness of existence itself, a theatrical play for manifesting all the potentials of existence, whereas the most creative possibility is that of self-oblivion, where we experience the entire existence as outward and alien to us, as something else, diminishing and restricting the divine consciousness to the point of alienating it from ourselves, forcing us to think that we can be born and die at the same time. Such is the consciousness of the soul in the body, mind and ego, for the duration of our physical life. Even then, it never loses contact with its own divine whole. This bond is saved in the form of intuition, inspiration, every time we believe there is 'something out there', in religion, in all the mystical states where we stumble upon the restrictions imposed on the body and mind. They seem the most appealing to us because they reflect our true nature, the one we had had prior to the birth in this body, and the one we will have after we die.

Therefore, with the birth of this physical body we did not begin to exist, but we, then, entered a state inferior to the one we had had before birth, back in the phase while we still were the pure consciousness of the soul, the divine consciousness. We then entered a state so limited by this physical body of ours, that it is exactly the state of death we fear so much. In this world we are as dead as we could be. *The whole matter works in reverse: we died by being born in this body, and we will be born after the physical death of the body.* Since the real death does not exist, there is not even the possibility of it occurring in existence, our state in this world is still closer to the dream-like state, as compared to which the consciousness of the soul is the big awakening, enlightenment or resurrection.

All true spiritual traditions testify to this.

The Egyptian *Book of the Dead* got this false name in the works of European translators. It does not speak of death no more than it speaks of the dead. Its original title is *The Book of Coming Forth by Day*. The process of the consciousness of the soul, upon the death of the physical body, which returns to itself into the light of divine existence, is what this book actually deals with. It is described like coming out of the dark into the light of the day. From a dream to an awakened state.

The Tibetan Book of the Dead reveals much the same story. The soul is faced with a *bright light*, with itself, with the divine, the greater part of itself that remained unembodied. However, the power of illusions acquired during life is still in effect, and if it remains unrecognized as a dream or an illusion, the consciousness of the soul keeps coming back to a new birth to strengthen the awareness of itself and become independent of the body's influence. When the consciousness of the soul grows so strong that the power of illusion the mind has in the body becomes so weak, at that point further incarnations in the body are no longer an option. Then, the cycle of reincarnations ends.

Bhagavad Gita, the divine song, stresses repeatedly that nobody is born and nobody dies. It is a description of the holographic universe, the divine existence which is the only reality.

Literally, all the folk traditions from all over the world, have some kind of a memory of the consciousness of the soul before birth.[16] Many of them celebrated death of a physical body as the return of the soul to itself, to its authentic state. Funerals were a legitimate reason for celebration. With the onset of Judeo-Christian beliefs, everything was turned upside down, and the civilization as we know it today was set in motion. It is the civilization that cultivates oblivion and materialization of the consciousness. It was necessary because no material culture would occur if people continued to nurture the consciousness of the soul aspiring to go back to their divine state. The consciousness of the soul is so strong and inviting that man besotted with it has no other material interests. However,

---

[16] There are numerous scientific studies on existence of the soul and reincarnation. Often the research scientists would embark on a quest as firm skeptics and materialists, in order to prove that no such thing as a soul exists, and the more thorough they did their research and gathered data, the more they were presented with evidence contrary to their initial point. Actually, all the scientists who began the research to debunk the soul and reincarnation myths, ended up as most fervent supporters of the idea of reincarnation, their additional claim was that they do not 'believe' in reincarnation, now they know. They were simply met with solid scientific evidence. The case of Ian Stevenson is the perfect example – he examined over 3000 reincarnation cases and had them well-documented in 12 books. The University of Virginia lectures Division of Perceptual Studies today. Research was further continued by Jim Tucker. Hypnotic regression appears to be the best tool for acquiring the detailed accounts of reincarnation stories, with additional evidence obtained by going out in the field after a hypnotic session to validate the findings and stories of clients. The pioneer on the field is Dr. Helen Wambach, who was also one of those who set out to overthrow the entire concept of reincarnation. Victor Zammit is one of those who were first the prosecutors of reincarnation, only to become a witness in its favor in the end. Probably the most famous name is Dr. Michael Newton with his research into hypnotic regression. The list goes on and on, with names like: Dr. Gerald Netherton, Dr. Arthur Guirdham, Dr. Varvara Ivanova, Peter Ramster and many more.

the plan for this world is for the consciousness of the soul to express itself in a creative way, to recognize all the possible states as divine ones, which they in their essence are. That is the overall process of materialization of consciousness of the soul, merging of the spiritual and material through the process of developing material culture and technology. That resulted in an even bigger oblivion of the consciousness of the soul. The world became a gigantic graveyard, both literally and metaphorically. All conflicts in this world have their origin in our lack of awareness of the consciousness of our soul, one same consciousness that is in everything as the primary source of everything. A body crucified on the cross became the idol to all the Christians. Fear of death became the foundation of the development of culture, and the idea of culture was reduced to mind programming. The only true culture is expressing the consciousness of the soul, the objective and true awareness of everything; everything else would fall under the category of mind programming. It is all a way for the divine consciousness to experience its ultimate limits, its supreme creativity in the form of being utterly oblivious of itself. It is identical to what all of us are trying to do in this world – experiencing the essence individually. Afterward, the only remaining option is the return to oneself. To the awakening.

Why the whole affair of being born and dying is turned upside down will become clear to us if we stop for a moment and remind ourselves of the nature of the divine reality, the Absolute, that it expresses itself through its opposition, 'the divine particle' which currently constitutes the overall existence. For that reason, the overall existence is a reflection of the exact opposite of the divine Absolute, of its reality. In that way, everything reflects in us as the miniature holographic fragment of the divine whole. We perceive existence opposite to what it really is. We as people exist so that it is overcome and returned once more to its original state, for the real awareness of the true nature of the divine reality to crystallize in us, first having gone through all the temptations experiencing all its oppositions. *We are the breaking point*. For that reason we can be aware of both sides, the real and the illusory one, of this world and beyond, of god and devil, good and evil, the manifested and the unmanifested reality. As regards the acquired experiences, our state is the most abundant. It is exactly for this reason that it is so hard. It is best depicted by a man crucified on the cross, the crucifix of the horizontal existence in this world and the vertical of the divine existence; halfway between human and divine; the conscious and the unconscious. Only after a crucifixion like that, the full awareness of the divine is made possible, but the full awareness of the human, as well. One should not cultivate the illusion that a crucifixion is a ritual which happened a long time ago, and serves a shallow purpose of being a symbol and religious inspiration today. No. Crucifixion is the life of every human being on this planet.

However, when we say we died when we were born in this body, and we are truly born only with the death of this body, it may seem like an invitation to die, as an act of glorifying death, to a mind which is always identified with the body and without sufficient connection to the consciousness of the soul. It is yet another illusion of the mind, though, of the consciousness eclipsed in the body, due to its inability to grasp the entire reality. This illusion grows strong in young and naive souls, who envisage spirituality as something that opposes materiality, as a means of escape from the real world into monasteries.

If the heart of the matter is that we were never born, the obvious conclusion is that death cannot present itself as any kind of solution or an ideal state, or salvation from a life filled with adversity. We cannot die. Wishing for death is a negation of life, and we know that only life exists, only existence exists. You cannot escape life by running to death. The only solution and salvation from suffering comes with the proper understanding of life. By understanding life, we begin to understand the consciousness of the soul, because it is one and the same thing. Upon understanding the consciousness of the soul we see that the entire life, the entire nature, is nothing but the projection of our soul, this whole world is our creation, our intelligent design. We become absorbed with the highest rapture and bliss upon seeing this world, when we start to view it with such consciousness of the soul, and when we begin to realize how much effort was put in creating everything we see around ourselves, all the living conditions in this world, how miraculous it all is, grand, powerful and worthy. It was us who engendered all of this in order to express ourselves. Naturally, not us the way we are in the body now, but as souls, as the over-souls of our individual souls, as the angels and archangels of god we created the entire cosmos and the life itself.

Any notion of death becomes pointless then!

Man who commits suicide bitterly regrets it when he makes a cross over to the other world, he experiences his mistake in a much harsher way than the worst moments of life he had had in this world.

Suicide is justified only as euthanasia, only when there really are no more conditions for life and when remaining in the body would become so negative as to jeopardize the consciousness of the soul. If death is indeed imminent, a conscious death is far better than torture, in that case. However, there have been other cases when such an anguish is needed for the sake of some experience, like facing one's misdeeds, for example. Therefore, it is extremely difficult to ascertain whether a suicide is justifiable or not. It is always better to test the limits by enduring the suffering and temptation, and simply observe what novel experience will come our way, than resolve the matter instantly based on some current mood. We are always a part of the learning process whilst still living, of course, not only in the way we solely desire, but more often than not, in a way we perceive to be unfavorable for us. It is because we cannot see the whole picture from our perspective. It may often be the case that things difficult and vile imposed on us, at long last, lead us to some good, to growing up much needed we would never consciously accept voluntarily. Hence, the temptation to commit suicide is in 99% actually a test in moving the limitations of our ego, mind and the comfort zone, the trying out of broadening one's perception and deeper understanding.

Taking part in this grandiose beauty and the perfection of existence has its price. The price for it is our suffering. Try to take the view on life like participating in some huge show, a big and expensive project which, apart from you, involves many people, too, on a grand stage, it is very crowded, someone pushes you, steps on your toe or hurts you, and you do not properly play your role. After the physical life the most excruciating pain will seem a lot less than it appeared during life, we will be happy for having paid the ticket and took part in this grandiose performance. We will suffer in this and the other world if we tried to avoid paying for it, if we tried to avoid taking part in life whatever it was like, because then, from the perspective of the soul, we will be able to see that absolutely every single life in this world is a reflection of the divine perfection of existence; not a single one is in vain or meaningless. The only true cause of suffering is refusing to live the life you have now.

With awareness like this, taking the lives of other beings (whether human or beast) becomes impossible.

When in this world man realizes the full awareness of his soul, it becomes absolutely impossible for him to jeopardize any kind of life, there is one consciousness in all of them, it is the same divine consciousness that conditions everything, all the life, it is the consciousness of the soul which in us. It sees itself in everything, it sees the one 'divine particle', the very divine Absolute. Therefore it is absolutely absurd and impossible for it to jeopardize anything. It can only manifest itself as the unity which is perceived as the unconditional divine love here. It can only heat, feed, teach and graciously look after all the beings. It can never negate or reject anyone ever.

SIN: THE PERFECT REASON
FOR THE BIRTH AND DEATH

There is one important detail about reincarnation, which explains why souls reincarnate in the body in the first place, why they come back into this world. All those who experienced a near death experience (NDE), and those who brought into awareness the state between two lives in a hypnotic regression, testify of recapitulation when they went over their entire lifetime, every moment of their lives, but all at once, without time as a reference point. However, they did not only see the things they did/committed, they equally experienced with the same sense of involvement how the other parties experienced that and what effect it had on them. Everything we did to others we see both ways, from our point of view, but from the perspective of all the other people in the event, as well. Additionally, they saw all their actions from a higher perspective, why they happened the way they did, and what different options were available, what possible changes it could have made. They saw what they should have done, but did not, and that hurt a lot. They realize to what a degree they were restricted within the confinements of the body, how subjective they were in their states and deeds, although the consciousness of our being is objective, perfect and omnipresent. They are able then to perceive events from the perspective of divine consciousness, and analyze the life plan of the individual consciousness which was present in the body. The mistakes and setbacks torment the soul of man, cause unease and immediate need for repair, for repentance.

This is why the soul itself makes a decision to go back to a life where it will be able to finalize the maturing process and become better. To be better in a sense *to enable the divine consciousness to become aware of itself albeit the rigid limiting conditions of the physical body, to become aware of its unlimited absolute nature. That is the real purpose of rebirths, reincarnations*. The soul makes an informed decision, nobody coerces it into anything.

Not only will we remember absolutely everything after the death of the body, because there is nothing that can disappear in existence, but we will equally clearly remember all those things we do not wish to be reminded of. And we will go back to mend our ways, to right our wrongs. This is the reason why we were born here, because of the memory of everything, because of our sins. It is a better option then, to stop ourselves from making mistakes now. We cannot escape from ourselves because universe is a hologram, whatever we do to others we, actually, do to ourselves, everything is merely an expression of one single 'divine particle'.

Every man, sooner or later, repents. When he exhausts all the karmic possibilities going down the wrong path he starts to realize that he is in a blind alley and he wishes to find the right way with all his heart. All people repent. There is no need for them to be forced into anything, but it may be of use for them to get reprimanded to start going back before hitting rock bottom. Experiencing your lowest point in life is always an IQ test, more accurately, finding out how open your mind is for the consciousness of the soul. Warning signs are all around. Some people need more lives to realize that and repent. Many big and important experiences require a drama that has more acts, more lifetimes. It should not concern us if some sinner gets away with murder without 'punishment' for his wrongdoings. You have not seen the ending of the story yet. The windmills of God grind slowly.

However, forces that keep people in an unconscious state have twisted the story upside down and convinced people that they are 'sinners' just because they exist, because they made an effort to be conscious, since they ate from 'the tree of knowledge'.

The word that keeps being translated throughout the entire New Testament as 'repentance' is the Greek word 'metanoia' which means the *metamorphosis of consciousness*. The Greek article 'meta' is found in a number of Greek words, such as metaphore, metaphysics, metamorphosis. According to that, the article 'meta' indicates a transition, or transformation, or otherworldly properties.

The other part of the word that is translated as repentance - *noia* – is a derivative of the Greek word *nous*, which means mind/consciousness. Therefore the word *metanoia* in its essential meaning denotes the transformation of consciousness, the transcendence of mind (identical to the teaching of Buddha and Patanjali in Yoga Sutras). However, in Christian church the idea of the transcendence of mind, *metanoia*, was destroyed by twisting it to the exact opposite teaching about 'repentance' which supports the idea of the eternal sinfulness of humans owing to which negative emotions are stimulated in them. The truth is that with such a suggestion humans are encouraged to be sinners. Indeed, there is no religion with so much violence like Christianity, which teaches man to be sinful. It is only a scare tactic that generates a victim mentality and slavelike mindset in order to maintain the authoritative church hierarchy.

The Biblical tree of knowledge is the tree whose branches are in the sky and leaves are on the ground, the tree that branches out from the divine consciousness into the over-souls and individual souls. Therefore, 'to eat from the tree of knowledge' means to have the perception of consciousness of the soul, the divine consciousness, our true origin. Twisting this truth upside down and the conviction that we are 'born sinners' could be accepted because it is based on the fundamental truth all people are partially intuitively aware of, that they were born here because they were not conscious enough in their previous life, they had made a mistake. The Christian church transformed the expression *to do wrong* to the noun *wrongdoing*. Exile from Eden is the description of becoming oblivious of one's true, divine nature. Feeling bad because of some failure in the previous incarnation and the reason to return to a new birth, Judeo-Christianity augments into 'suffering from hell'. There is no hell. There is only heaven on earth waiting for us to return to it as conscious beings. Hell can exist only in an unconscious man, as his state of consciousness. Ignorance is the only evil in the holographic universe.

HOW FAR ARE WE FROM PERFECTION
OR: WHY ARE PEOPLE SO ABNORMAL

The projection of divine consciousness of itself in the form of souls, that try out all the possibilities of the divine existence, does not take place mechanically and monotonously. It is a long and complex process.

The awareness of all the possibilities souls are able to experience while finding the true meaning of existence, which they will retrieve to the divine through themselves, is such a daunting and intricate process that cannot be finalized in one take, in one life. One soul is not big enough for the task either, and that is why there are so many of them. Actually, one over-soul splits itself into a myriad of individual souls. The same way one principle creates all the stars, and each star radiates innumerable rays of light all round.

Naturally, this multitude along with everything else is just imagination of one divine consciousness which through one 'divine particle' expresses everything that exists.

For the same reason more souls than one are needed, each soul has more than one life in the body, multiple incarnations. The reason for this is the magnitude and complexity of the task.

Since accomplishing the task in only one lifetime is mission impossible, in order for the man to completely bring all the possibilities of divine existence into awareness and retrieve this consciousness to the divine, upon his death, he does not go back to his original divine state. He merely exits the body and goes to a higher dimension, the higher astral and lower mental world, which has its title in religions as the 'heavenly world'. He there recapitulates all his experiences and goes back to the physical world to continue the process of becoming aware of all the possibilities of existence.

This is appropriately depicted in the following picture.

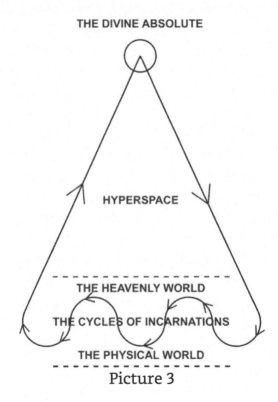

Picture 3

Consciousness of the soul projects itself into an individual physical body. It is perpetually born in it and returns to the heavenly world as many times as necessary until it learns its lesson and matures to the point it can no longer lose the consciousness of itself, the divine consciousness, which it then sees in every living form, so that yet another birth would seem redundant. The cycle of reincarnation ends and the soul reunites with its source, the divine Absolute.

The number of reincarnations depends on the consciousness of the soul while it still resides in the body. When the soul commences the incarnation cycle it is immature and appears young. The soul itself does not have age like the body, because it does not exist in time. The only thing that is young about it is its experience in/with this world. Souls that have had multiple lives experienced more and that is why we call them old and mature souls.

Young souls are easy to spot by their inexperience and the fact that they find it hard to manage things, the youngest ones are incapable of making a home for themselves, they live in huts, they do not know how to do the simplest things in life, how to organize anything, they do not see the real nature of events and are therefore, in great need of learning from experience and repeating lessons. Similar to rearing children. The only difference is we are talking about adult people here, even entire nations and races. Some are more advanced and mature, more diligent and successful in their work, while others are not and require much effort to learn the basic things. A mature and experienced soul gets to the heart of the matter instantly, it 'reads' events at a glance, its maturity is best expressed through its impeccable work ethics, it is very practical, efficient and creative. It does not require much coaching, it needs the basic information about what needs to be done, and it will do it, there is no need for anyone to push it.

Character of young souls is the exact opposite of this. They learn the harder way. Everything that is done

wrongly and harmfully in this world, young and immature souls are the ones to do it. They can be violent, too.
The violence immature souls are capable of does not come
from their intrinsic evil trait. No man is evil in his essence. He cannot be if he has a soul. Evil deeds are committed by people only because they are unconscious,
identified with the ostensible reality of the physical
world, because they do not have a well-developed consciousness of the soul. They are forced to struggle for survival at all costs. This makes them violent. They do not
see or know anything else, only what their physical
senses instruct them to perceive. The more they see
themselves as a physically isolated individual, the more
they experience the outer world as hostile, contrary to
their own interests. The more they are alienated from
their soul, the more they are in conflict with the world.
When a large number of such unconscious individuals
congregate, they always spontaneously find a reason to
start a fight. All debates and quarrels people engage in
stem form the lack of awareness of the true nature of reality, unconscious people try to explain and impose on
others what they know or think they know. All the people
talk and argue in order to show what exists in this world,
the different viewpoint of this one same world. They do
not see that everything is an expression of divine consciousness, that everything is perfect. They are unable to
see that there is an identical consciousness of the soul in
them and in every other being. They are trying to find
their way through various religious teachings that try to
inspire them to comprehend divine existence, to realize
that the physical world and the physical body they have
is not everything that there is, that 'something higher' exists, and that is why they have to be good. When through
the newly imposed ethics and discipline they become

good, at least a little, they become convinced it is the right way to awareness and understanding. But their impulse is to start projecting all of that into some God, or a religious authority, instead of recognizing this understanding as the nature of consciousness and the perfection of the very existence.

Therefore, conflicts between people do not actually exist, the same way that conflicts between souls are not possible because they know they are a reflection of one same divine consciousness. All conflicts are caused because of the varying states of consciousness in people, of different individual experiences of consciousness.

All conflict between people can be overcome only with the understanding of what it is that joins them together in one perfect whole, by understanding the consciousness of the soul, the divine consciousness that facilitates them all.[17]

From an objective point of view, we are all emanations of one and the same divine consciousness, we are leaves of the same tree. One identical divine consciousness is divided in every man for it to be able to express all the potential aspects of the experience of existence. How

---

[17] A big number of conflicts in this world could be overcome only with the proper understanding and dialogue. The perfection of a cultured dialogue, which includes understanding the consciousness of the soul and divine consciousness, was introduced by Plato, through Socrates' dialogues. He proved that the correct understanding of the world itself and between people is not possible without the proper understanding of the nature of the soul. Socrates' Daimon is the higher mind that connects us with the consciousness of the soul. We all, in one way or another, search for the correct understanding in this world, whereas misunderstandings and conflicts are many. Nobody reads Plato today. There will be a more refined dialogue and understanding in this world when Plato's works become the most important subject in school.

absurd it is for the leaves on the tree to fight with one another! The awareness of this would remove every conflict that exists between people. We all contribute to the better understanding of existence, it is so big and complex that one conscious subject is not enough for everything to be known. It takes a myriad of conscious subjects to do the task, a great many people. They are all working on the same task in order to achieve the same goal.

Conflicts between people are a reflection of perfection and lead in the direction towards it. Through conflict, illusions are expressed, and it is easier to become aware of them; to get rid of them. Conflict is a catharsis that liberates us from the illusions. After every conflict and suffering we realize it was merely a harder way to learn some truth. At the end of every conflict we see that we could have been smarter.

The additional problem is created by the strong pull of the divine consciousness that has the same attractive effect both on the young and the old souls, because the divine consciousness is omnipresent and the source of everything. Old souls recognize and distribute it in a correct way, through unconditional love and understanding, teaching and aiding all beings, by harmonizing with it on all the planes of existence. However, the allurement of the divine consciousness can be expressed in a highly deviant way in both the young and the old souls. They may commit the most atrocious misdeeds thinking they serve God that way. The stupidest ones will wrap explosives around them and go to a mall, to offer their sacrifice to God by killing the 'infidels' – instead of doing exactly the same in the church that instructed them to do this. It is becoming for the most immature souls to do the exact opposite of what they should; to take life thinking they serve it, to kill divine consciousness instead of expressing it here on earth. This is the reason we came to planet earth: to experience the divine in all its aspects, and not to fight the aspects of divine emanations we do not understand.

When man kills in the name of God it is utmost opposition point of the manifestation of the divine consciousness, the darkest corner of existence. It presents the ultimate absurd in the universe, because only God exists, everything else is an illusion. However, from that point onward the greatest submission to God is possible. Much like pulling an elastic rope, when it is at its maximum stretch, at its ultimate distance point from the original state, when the movement in the opposite direction is at its peak, then the power for the return to the initial state is the strongest. This is the paradox that defines the entire existence. It appears as though God plays yoyo with itself.

All the negativity young and immature souls do in this world can fall under the category of a lack of making sense as to why they came in to this world in the first place. They constantly try to learn in all possible and impossible ways. They cannot comprehend that they came into this world as a helping hand to support God's creation, to manifest concretely and practically the creative consciousness, that is why our hands were designed to be the perfect tools, that would further create other tools. This was what they were doing before birth, as souls they practiced creating various living forms on different planets. In this physical world they should just continue doing that, doing anything, because every kind of work is equally valuable, from gardening to cleaning streets and building a satellite in space. We would have little use of satellite technology if we did not have a garden to enjoy and streets that are squeaky-clean. Miners dug out a met-al the satellite was made of, farmers fed the scientists that designed it. It is all one joint process of sustaining the livelihood and work. Due to their connectedness everybody's work is equally important. Without one worker the others fail. Only our unconsciousness and inability to see things from the perspective of the wider whole drive us to disrespect somebody's work, to regard something as less valuable, or unfavorable. It is only because we are unaware of the wider perspective, of the perfect whole.

Instead of working in this world immature souls generally try to go back to the original divine state, they always feel exists, albeit vaguely. The more spiritual ones escape the world by going to a monastery. The less spiritual ones steal, look for 'easy money' so that they can enjoy.

The entire conflict on this planet can be defined as the conflict between souls who are aware of the need to go forward, and the plan they came to this world for, should be finalized, and the divine consciousness should be directed into all the physical shapes of this world, and 'Kingdom Come' should be placed on earth – and, on the other hand, there are immature souls who are unaware of all of that, but have some naive and intuitive notion that they originate from the divine consciousness and feel limited and restricted in this hostile environment. They just want to go back, or at least to dream of the divine. For the young and immature souls it is a natural and logical state of functioning and reasoning. They went on to create their own culture and religions which only serve to resist this world, to 'save their soul', but actually, to escape an unpleasant task they had set themselves, and that is to go through an education, a hard school by the name of Planet Earth and manifest the divine consciousness on it through their own work and presence. Islam, Hinduism and Orthodox Christianity are all examples of such religions and cultures. They interpret quite accurately the divine and keep the consciousness of their soul, but they do not serve the purpose they came to this world for. They move the development of consciousness backward, rather than forward, they enable people to remain childish rather than mature. Although they keep inside them the highest knowledge of the nature of the divine in a human soul, their practical application of this knowledge in this world is with poor results.

Judeo-Christianity which is expressed through the Protestant culture, especially Calvinism, and freemasonry, are the best teachers to people of what their real purpose in this world is, which is work and expansion of consciousness. This type of spirit built the modern Western civilization. By all means, they do this within certain boundaries that are neither all-inclusive nor perfect. They lack all the depth of consciousness of the soul. But so far, they have been able to pull this off in one way or another. It is a big mistake to expect human growth to be ideal and absolute. One should be realistic and understand what is feasible, what can be done regarding space and time of the given circumstances.

This process is a two-way thing: historically, outwardly and collectively – and within man, individually. Historically, outwardly and collectively man is undergoing a developing phase, and we are still in the first part of that phase. Existence of aristocracy and its ownership over the corporations proves we are still in The Middle Ages, the only difference is we have electricity, whereas human rights and freedoms do not exist in the most developed countries, we are in a trial and error stage regarding that. Within the man, the entire process is best reflected in his maturity and ability to be realized regardless of space and time, and events taking place in the real world, here and now. Therefore, the outer and the inner expressions of the process, should under no circumstances, be confused. Outwardly, he still has not grown sufficiently, and the growing pains may take a while, it is a slow and lengthy historical process, whereas inwardly man is able to realize himself in his entirety through self-knowing. It works independently from one another, although it may go hand in hand in the sense that it stimulates or stunts the growth. For example, conscious people enhance the civilizational progress, but the existing limitations of civilizational development restrict people living in such a system.

The equal imbalancement exists in those forces that push the human development forward, through work and learning. They, also, do not have the right sense of measure and insight into the purpose of what they do, so some of them, especially the free masons, are ready to walk over dead bodies just to get ahead. A much greater effort is needed for creation than destruction, for destruction all that is required is letting go and inertia will do the rest, like sliding downward, for creativity serious investing of energy is required, like climbing uphill. It is hard to determine whose effort prevails in that destruction, whether it is of those who pull forward or those who want to go back to heaven, or to have everything exactly as it is, provided it suits them enough. Their tug-of-war is also expressed in the form of all the wars and clashes between civilizations in this world. They do not see that they need each other as a complementary quality. Technological development without the consciousness of the soul could turn this world into a form sophisticated hell. On the other hand, the consciousness of the soul cannot express itself in any limited way, without the type of development that involves the technological progress. Only when the consciousness of the divine is realized through the material culture and work, only then will it be fully realized in this world. It is the goal of every civilization and culture – to unite the consciousness with existence.

We exist in this world because of this imbalance in the process of raising awareness. Were we perfect the way we were, we would have never been born here in the first place. A large percentage of souls on planet earth is actually made up of the young and immature souls. That is why this world is the way it is.

Thankfully, young souls that are so immature as to do evil are the minority (if they were majority, we would be in a serious trouble). Most young souls are aware of the fact that they do not know everything and they are willing to learn, to grow, to rejoice and enjoy every kind of work and development, building something new and better. Improving the conditions of living unites them with the consciousness of the soul and the divine. That is why they love creative jobs and personal growth. Such souls advance at the highest pace in their karmic maturing in this world. They are always positive, possess a sense of humor, and have healthy interests, enthusiasm, they enjoy learning, the fight for justice. Still, they are not enlightened and can suffer for a number of reasons.

What we should know additionally regarding incarnations and karmic growth of the souls we will learn if we remind ourselves that this divine consciousness is timeless, and that is why it manifests its holographic universe currently through all the parallel realities. It all happens in a timeless present, and not over a course of time. Time is merely a way for the three-dimensional reality to manifest, and apart from it there are other dimensions as well, where time progressively diminishes and finally disappears into ether. In this original, most refined state of reality everything is merged into One (Samadhi). It means that in reality everything happens in one timeless unity, that all the possibilities are manifested across the parallel realities, currently, meaning timelessly. Therefore our incarnations do not play out over the course of time, in a linear way, one after another, they happen all at once and they have already happened, but in parallel realities. Our mind is tied to the idea of time and the linear three-dimensionality and has an illusion of things happening along a set timeline, one physical life of ours has its beginning at birth and the end with the death of the body, which are all conditions of a 3D world, based on which the mind concludes that outside the body it must be the same, that the higher dimensions also have time as such. It is an illusion. All our incarnations are currently taking place at the present moment. One over-soul divides itself into several souls, and every soul can split itself into multiple physical incarnations. Why would the soul waste time in linear rebirthing from one body to another when in its essence it is timeless, when everything is made up of one timeless 'divine particle' and when everything co-exists in parallel realities?

Actually, were we more careful in our attempt to understand this in its entirety, it would become clear to us that all our incarnations have already taken place, although they are actively happening as we speak. Since they have already happened, our current reality we are just dreaming of in a state of deep sleep. We have been, on numerous occasions, told that life is a dream, an illusion, *maya*. Buddha instructed us to wake up, there is no need to do anything else, and he showed us how.

Still, it would be easier to understand this if we compared incarnations with our process of everyday sleeping and the state of being awake. The only difference is that when we wake up in the morning we have memory of our current life and continuity. When the body dies and we are born again a disruption in the continuity happens, at least for the physical mind in the body, which is logical since it is a different body so there is no continuity in memory. We need, in this current life of ours, continuity in space and time because of the possibility of acquiring experiences and designing, comprehending all the available options. If we were aware of all the parallel realities here, of all our incarnations, there would be chaos. Life would not be possible.

Our rhythm of life made up of states of being awake and sleeping is actually a reflection of the rhythm of incarnations, of being born and dying, because reality is a holographic projection, every tiny detail of it reflects the image of the whole. The same principle can be applied to our life in the physical body, it reflects the principles of incarnations, the way in which our soul exists in the absolute sense.

We are intuitively aware of these parallel incarnations of ours, because we keep swapping information between them which enhances our growth. Actually, this is the best way for us to learn. Whenever we choose to experience one option in life, all the other parallel incarnations of ours select other options. Truth be told, that is the only way for us to gain awareness of all the possibilities that are out there. This gathering of experience is not the same in all the parallel incarnations, consequently, there is a central incarnation that encapsulates them all. It resembles one head with the brain inside, that governs the entire body with different limbs.

While we are still insufficiently aware in the body, we receive information from other parallel incarnations unconsciously, via dreams and visions, through sudden impulses of inspiration. Once we finally awaken to the consciousness of the soul, we see all our parallel possibilities and lives and we realize that it is all a perfectly coordinated, synchronized system designed for us to live and learn in. We exited the illusion of time and identification with only one body. That is the reason why we can no longer be born again. But we have the option to live the way we please. For the first time ever. It is a paradox, that we have our own will and freedom for the first time once we strip ourselves of the illusions of life, and we can live our life only when we no longer need it. At that point we have maturity and the maximum insight into reality and divine consciousness of the soul. Unfortunately, we have also been given the freedom to gain the insight in a much harder and more painful way.

THE PERFECTION OF SUFFERING

The basic reason why there is suffering in this world is because we keep resisting reality unconsciously and unreasonably, reality in general, but also the type of reality that constitutes our current situation, our state and development.

We resist the reality of existence itself because we do not see how perfect everything is every moment of every day, cosmos could not exist if it were not exactly the way it is now. Our personal reality is also a part of this perfection, it, too, belongs to cosmos, but it is prone to change and this option of modification is the reflection of perfection, as well. Perfection would not be perfect if it did not allow for every kind of change, both favorable and unfavorable. It would be a perfect prison then.

We experience suffering because we are unaware of perfection, and we are unaware because we are restricted in the physical body, our perception is limited, hence the resistance to reality. This resistance generates pain and suffering. The reality is not to blame, our resistance is. It is natural to feel pain when you hit something. There is no blame on the part of the wall if we hit our head against it and it hurts. Reality can never be the cause of suffering because reality conditions everything, ourselves included, therefore it can never present a contradiction in/to itself. Otherwise, it could not be the reality that conditions everything. There is no such thing as a wrong reality.

We resist reality because we do not understand it and we do not perceive it correctly, we do not see that it always and in totality supports us with unconditional love. It conditions everything so it will even support our resistance of itself. We are free to focus ourselves on anything we choose, either a positive or a negative goal, we will always be supported by the divine whole because we are its conscious subjects who are here for the purpose of experiencing everything that can be experienced. However, we will not get the support for the ultimate negative consequences. There is a measure to how much support we deserve. We have been granted the option of freedom only as a tool to experiment with, not as a tool for the total destruction. However, if we are limited and trapped in our illusions to the point of pursuing the negative option only, we will lose support of the whole and ruin our current incarnation. We will do this to ourselves. The soul will release the consciousness of such a mind where it is no longer able to have influence on, to run wild the way it sees fit. Those are the cases, often seen, where people are so self-destructive that nothing and nobody can put a stop to them. They can be experiments with the free will that may take several incarnations to wear off. It is useful to know that if we go overboard in this experimenting with the free will of mind/ego, it may take multiple incarnations to stop and repent, and it will be correspondingly more painful.

There are karmic plans for trying out the versatility of experience where several lives are included. We know them as cases where people die following their misconceptions and misdeeds, but seemingly needlessly and untimely.

It should be made clear that consciousness of the soul is discreet, whereas the consciousness of the mind is pushy. Consciousness of the soul inspires and invites implementing the positive methods only; consciousness of the mind imposes and uses all kinds of tricks and illusions. Mind has a body and senses for its ally, and when consciousness is reduced to them only it is relatively easy to be deceived and convinced that what the mind shows us, is the only truth that there is. That is why the road to suffering is always paved with good intentions, with very nice and appealing tile patterns, excellent advertising skills, and an invitation to enjoy a quick fix success. It is important to know that the bodily mind may lose the mercy of the soul, but only in cases when that is one of the ways for the man to become aware of his illusions. Young souls have a stronger consciousness of the body and mind and it often happens that the physical consciousness overpowers the consciousness of the soul. Then, the consciousness of the soul may withdraw and abandon the consciousness of the mind to have its way. They become the cases of the lowest kind of behavior in people, the world evil, that we, for a good reason, call soulless.

They are extreme cases of suffering. More often it happens that the cases of suffering are a consequence of not understanding that the consciousness of our higher mind and the consciousness of our soul do not permit the fulfillment of some low drives and cheap desires we may have along the way. It is a childish suffering because somebody did not fulfill our wishes. It is a relief to know that the reason for our unfulfilled desires lies in the fact that our higher mind does not permit it because it sees better than our physical mind where such a fulfillment would lead us to. It would often lead us to tragic consequences. Our soul had a set plan of experiences for us to go through before we were born. However, the physical mind acts like a child who sees something shiny in the store and wants to have it. The higher mind will not let it, to avoid wasting time on needless things and do itself some harm.

In such a way the divine consciousness always supports and safeguards us because everything is good and perfect. Only our limitations make us experience it as suffering.

This is the hardest to understand when human relationships are concerned. When we love and want someone, and he/she disappears from our life we suffer the most. However, at that point we do not see clearly the entire picture, who knows where the union with such a person would lead us to? Additionally, we fail to see the life plan and karma of the other person who has walked out on us. We have to respect that, and not just verbally brag about respecting other people's will and freedom of choice. If somebody decided to leave us, or leave the life on the earth plane, we should learn to respect that fact, and not merely feel miserable for our loss. Maybe someone who loved us, decided to abandon us because he/she has fulfilled their mission in our life, the right measure of presence, if he/she had stayed on, maybe our life plan would not have worked out the way it should. It would not be good for us, and maybe it would not be good for the other party, either. Many people suffer for being alone. Maybe they do not see what a hell they would have gone through with that other person. Solitude provides maximum freedom to work on oneself. Once we leave this world we would suffer for not making use of our time better, instead we suffered for something we do not actually need. We may go through experiences of losing somebody or something so that we can learn the proper way to live. Many souls were born just to make us suffer which will force us to wake up, to mend our ways and bring us back on the right path.

Perfection is at the foundation of life and people die when it is their time to go, in accordance with the plan of their soul. Additionally, following the same principle of that perfection which keeps manifesting itself in multiple dimensions, death is just the experience of being awakened to a higher life, not the cessation or the end of living. When somebody dies young, it only seems like a tragedy from our point of view. From the perspective of the soul, it is only a hasty return back to its essence, maybe the plan and the role to play for the current life were fulfilled. There are many incarnations where we play the supporting role so as to help a fellow being achieve its purpose, to go through certain experiences and learn something in this world; to cause an event to take place, some process to become finalized. Once the task has been fulfilled, the soul leaves this world. The purpose of reincarnations is not for the personal goals of an individual soul to be fulfilled, but for all other people to be assisted along their path. Life is a joint venture of souls. Various exchanges and interactions may take place here.

One of the most severe blows we can experience is an untimely death of the loved one. It first strongly attracts us to love him/her more than ourselves even, and we do not realize that what we fell for in him/her was the consciousness of the soul, which is the same like our consciousness. Then, once they pull us so close to them, the consciousness of the soul with its sudden departure, backing off like in a judo fight, hits us on the ground of reality. It all teaches us to value and see in everything only the consciousness of the divine soul. It is a quick and brutal karmic lesson for those who are overly identified with the body.[18]

It is a brutal lesson intended for very few people who need it. The death of a loved one has other aspects to it, as well. Maybe a person died to avoid turning our life into hell later on. We should not judge based on what we do not know. A death like that would also be in harmony with the general picture of perfection, where everything is the way it should be.

Early death crystallizes the consciousness of the soul better and faster than joyous living to a ripe old age. A very long life may make a man lazy and disoriented. A comfortable and pleasant life also. You know what old, complacent people can be like. A very long life becomes more of a negation of life, and its opposition, than anything else. For that reason many lives were brought to an abrupt stop for the purpose of practicality and mental hygiene. We have been deprived many other things in life for the same reason.

Therefore, death as a cause of suffering should be dismissed if we want to understand that everything is perfect.

In reality, death is the best ally of humans in the process of awareness and awakening. Nothing in this world can give us more decisiveness, willpower, sincerity

---

[18] Very truly I tell you, unless a kernel of wheat falls to the ground and dies, it remains only a single seed. But if it dies, it produces many seeds. Anyone who loves their [physical -IA] life will lose it, while anyone who hates their life in this world will keep it for eternal life [the consciousness of the soul-IA]" (Holy Bible, NIV, John, 12: 24-25.) Whoever wants to save their soul in the physical body only, will not be able to do so. Whoever stops identifying with the body and becomes aware of the consciousness of their soul, will save themselves.

and clarity like the inevitability of death. Faced with death, we have our life entirely in our hands and there is no point in trying to escape into any illusions. Only in the face of death we give our best, our essence. That is why it is so attractive to us. However, in the context of the consciousness of the soul, in reality, there is no death, there is only a mind identified with the body. We manifest our best characteristics not because of death, but because of the proximity of the consciousness of the soul, because we, then, overcome the illusions of the body and mind. When we grow nearer to the experience of dying, the fear is gone, it only exists when we watch it from far away. We intuitively but clearly see that on the other side of death we will encounter our deeds and misdeeds. That is the root of the fear: that we did not do what we should have done, that we wasted time on useless things and illusions that we did what we should not have done. Using the religious terminology here: we fear facing our guardian angel who will condemn us for all our misdeeds. That is what startles us the most as regards death. We wise up instantly, and not because of the physical death itself. We are actually never afraid of the physical death. We are always afraid of the truth of our own lives.

Only to the physical mind the situation of overcoming the bodily limitations and illusions appears like death. Mind will use all its options and powers to try to avoid it, all the way from the very rational means to the very irrational ones. Following his mind, man would rather kill to save itself. When the consciousness of the soul is stronger, people chose to sacrifice themselves in order to save others. Anyone who chose to kill was actually distancing themselves from the consciousness of his soul.

One of the sources of suffering is old age, not only for those who are already old, but for young people who are beginning to age and experience fear of growing old and dying. Old age, too, is the picture of perfection, even more so than being young, although it is hard to see it before you grow older and mature. Every age of man has its characteristics, its perfections to be enjoyed, each entailing a deeper state of self-awareness. Youth is for enjoying fervor and passions, and old age is in the cognition of why there are passions in the first place, and what we have experienced through them. As old age draws closer to the consciousness of the soul, the older one is, and the more mature they are, the more open they are to higher dimensions, that propel the entire nature into existence, and which are internal to the human, because they are comprised of all the dimensions of nature. The more open he becomes for the higher dimensions, the more he is open for comprehending the entire nature and life itself, as well as for the empathy and compassion, for intuitive consciousness that originates from the connection with the higher mind and consciousness of the soul. That is why older people are, if they are any normal, naturally more religious, spiritual, kind and with more empathy and understanding. They are like this because they are closer to their soul. That is why they are closer to children, because children, too, are close to their soul. Old people are close to the consciousness of the soul because their life is at the end, and children are close to the consciousness of their soul because they recently came from that consciousness and into the body. The spiritual old men resemble children, they are free from the illusions of life so much so that they appear childish. For the same reason small children sometimes leave the impression of old age and wisdom with some gestures or insight. In both cases maturity comes from the proximity of the consciousness of the soul. The most mature old people find their sole comfort only in the beauty of nature and the purity of a child's soul, still untainted by the karmic contents and life dramas. More and more, they recognize the consciousness of the divine soul in the very nature and existence. That is the perfection of old age.

One additional cause of suffering may take place when a mature soul experiences stronger pull of the objective consciousness and begins to learn faster than it can take. Such acceleration of speed may bring experiences that teach the soul in the body faster that it is not just the body. Unfortunately, this world is a practical school where you learn by applying your knowledge practically, in order to acquire the direct experience, and the maturity of that kind may be served to us through an experience of death of a loved one, when any bond we had previously had to life becomes empty and insufficient, through the experience of one's own death or at least its vicinity, when all the life plans fall through, when a series of brutal events sets the soul free from the identification and attachment to the body and the world, he or she does not have to die, only to rise in understanding. In accordance with the general principle of the manifestation of everything that can be manifested, we must be brought to this understanding in all ways possible. The complete freedom of choice exists there. The previous metaphor of resisting reality by hitting oneself against the wall, can be changed to a different metaphor of being tied down to a horse who keeps pulling us all over the ground to the finish line. We will achieve our goals this way, as well, except it will be a lot more painful. This horse needs to be mounted, broken, and nothing in this world should be taken too seriously.

The proper speed is what it takes to mature successfully. On the one hand, our mind cannot accept an experience it is not sufficiently mature for, which it has been offered, it may even have come across it, which possessed and took it along, like the horse from our metaphor. On the other hand, the mind has a very powerful imagination which may develop the taste for experiences it is not mature enough for, that would from the perspective of the higher mind provide it with the negative results, and for that reason the higher mind prevents them. In both cases the mind due to its limitations cannot see straight away why that happens, why something pulls it and where it would lead to, and that is why it does not get what it wants, it does not realize why it has been blocked. One is like flooring the gas pedal and the other one acts like a brake. To drive safely through life one should be acquainted with both functions. All it takes is to recognize them in good time, in the way described here.

All experiences we have been offered in life, more than anything, require our enjoyment. Maybe you have not noticed because of some commotion, but this world was made for pleasure. This is the reason why it is so beautiful. If you were in possession of the consciousness of the soul with which you would be able to observe clearly, you would realize that every cubic inch of this world was the perfect beauty and creativity. A reflection of the divine perfection. It cannot be anything other than that. That is why people can find pleasure in the worst possible experiences and it is difficult to talk them out of it. It is all about enjoyment, we just cannot see where it takes us.

Although the beauty of this world is a reflection of its perfection, it was made for enjoyment for the sake of perception, awareness, the complete cognition of the essence of life, and not for the satisfaction of the lower drives. There must be some attraction to it, the state of being interested. However, young souls often confuse attraction for the sake of awareness with the attraction towards passion. Their process of maturing boils down to understanding why this world is so beautiful, for them to reach the answer that it is beautiful because it is a reflection of the divine consciousness of our soul, to be able to find the reason for its beauty in themselves, in their own soul.

As regards the suffering which is an accompanying element of growing up they should know that this world is designed in such a way so as not to allow the souls to identify too much with the outer objects, with the contents of this world. That is why life is transient, unstable and more than anything painful. If it were not so, if the human physical mind were able to find stronghold in the objects of the world, it would never make a turning for its source, toward the consciousness of the soul. It would remain so thoroughly enslaved within the confinement of this world completely infatuated with it, meaning its self-satisfaction, nothing would be able to wake it up, it would stay unconscious. To prevent that from happening, human life is designed in such a way that he keeps receiving blows to the head that wake him up, which take from him everything he comes by, which smash any idea he may have of safety, of any illusory feeling of sanctuary in this world, which reveal there is a lot more than meets the eye, that everything he sees is not everything that there is, and that is why he should never stop, he should always be open for new experiences, man has no safe haven in this world, he should go looking for 'eternal life' only.

Giving and taking the objects of desire has been carefully programmed to meet the right measure: first he is given them to know that they exist, and then it is taken away from him to prevent attachment, and identifying too much with the objects. We suffer because we do not follow the rhythm that serves the consciousness of the soul, the rhythm of give and take, until we come to the point of real understanding of its existence. The reason, therefore, is to stop searching for haven in the contents and objects of this world because it is only our reflection, it serves us, and that is why we should not serve it. The world exists for us and not vice versa, we do not exist for the world, the world is looking for its haven in us, and that is why we cannot find haven and understanding in the world – except to a very small degree, barely enough to show us the point of understanding as such, the meaning that is always connected with the consciousness of our soul. Every purpose and every joy we find in this world is connected to the consciousness of the soul, and not to this world, it merely served as means for the knowing of the consciousness of the soul, the divine consciousness. This world is just the means, and not the ends. However, it is so huge, so miraculous and perfect as means that we can easily mistake it for the goal.

The whole world is carefully designed so that we can live naked in it, like children in heaven, like some 'primitive' tribes live to this day. The whole world is our body, the real body we live in, and this physical body should just provide us with that experience. The fact that we are physically separated into a multitude of individual bodies, minds and experiences, should by no means fool us that we are one individual lost in a hostile world. Although that illusion is strong and effective for most of those 'individuals', one should know that it is merely an attitude of a schizophrenic mind. No more than that. However, thanks to the basic principle of the manifestation of the Absolute, the perfect freedom where everything-that-is can manifest itself as everything-that-can-be, this schizophrenic mind created its lifestyle which is predominant in the world today. However, because of this freedom everything can change, and this change depends on us alone.

Therefore, the coercion to awaken is one of the reasons for the perfection of suffering.

Perfection of suffering is best understood in the context of young and old souls. They all have their difficulties and tasks to learn and do.

Young souls have difficulties in learning and adapting to life in this world. Because of them there are all the laws and sanctions, a system of coercion and pressure. They, like small children, need discipline and coercion in order to learn the rules of this world. Since the consciousness of the soul is very strong, and because of that power it is hard to understand the principle of acquiring all kinds of experiences that exist in this world, young souls are hard to motivate to learn new rules. Because of the strong influence of the consciousness of the soul they wish to go back to the consciousness of the soul, to the innocence of sheer existence. Due to this resistance many difficulties arise, and the suffering for young souls, because they come in conflict with the challenges and limitations of this world. They do not see the wholeness of existence, the higher dimensions, the entire chain of causality, and events seem chaotic and illogical to them, they try to change them the way they know how, which is often limited and wrong. For that reason they must learn on experiences, and learning on one's own experiences automatically means learning on your mistakes. That is why all the adversity and suffering happens in this world for the young souls. More accurately: all the suffering and trouble in this world are caused by young souls who make problems in their learning. There is no suffering outside it as some objective state of affairs, as reality.

Old souls have a different kind of problem. They must learn to develop tolerance regarding the folly of the young souls. In that way they prove practically the presence of their higher consciousness, the awareness of the wholeness and the perfection of everything. Tolerance is a practical application of the higher, transcendental consciousness of the soul, in reality on the lower planes of existence. Life is always practical, your knowledge is in vain if you do not test and apply it practically. Namely, the mind is ability to view virtually every kind of reality from all kinds of aspects, and without its presence, irrelevant of space and time. That is why the mind is a very good tool for knowing the reality, but due to this perfection the mind provides us with the illusion that reality is already accomplished although it is only virtually imagined. People find it hard to distinguish between reality and illusion, between their mind. For that reason mind brings both reality and illusion. Without a clear mind we cannot become aware in this world, likewise, without the transcendence of the mind we cannot begin to scope the reality itself that surpasses this world and all the senses.

After an insight becomes clear to us we always have to prove it in practice, in real life. We often see that as a resistance to our knowing, it spoils our mood and tempts us needlessly, because it forces an exam and test upon us. However, it is all about the shifting of the level of consciousness. When we cross the threshold to a higher level, we immediately face its new conditions and challenges we have previously been unaccustomed to. That is all. The problem is that the crossing of this threshold toanother level of awareness we see as something abstract, fictional, much like everything else, which follows the old set patterns, and thus we are startled by the actual reality of this new level. That is why all the temptations we experience are merely compulsions to transition, to change. Every higher level is a higher reality. Only on the lowest level the consciousness is close to the illusions and fiction, the immature attitude toward reality. As we grow and uplift we must become more realistic and responsible.

We actually enjoy the perception of all the possibilities of existence. It is the primary intention of life and divine consciousness, to experience itself through us as conscious subjects. When we are the less conscious subjects we experience the overall possibilities of existence as primitive and spontaneous, and then we go through an ordeal. If we are more conscious subjects we experience all the possibilities in a noble and conscious manner, and every option we view as the meaning of existence.

There is no conflict between good and evil in this world, only a measure of the presence of consciousness of the soul and its absence in the mind and body of man. We should not fight evil, we should just battle our unconsciousness. By fighting evil, in accordance with the law of attraction, we merely fuel the idea of evil. (There are religious institutions that have a myriad of ways of inducing our struggle against evil and wickedness, with this they indirectly produce evil themselves.) We should just bring consciousness into all the experiences, without making choices, adding soulfulness, meaning the understanding the soul has of this world, widening the perception onto all the dimensions. The very consciousness of the soul will decrease the need for negative experiences and make this world a better place. This world is bad only if we limit it with our limited perception. Evil can only be conquered by good, hatred with love, conflicts with understanding.

Existence continues to refract itself across several dimensions, but we do not see all the dimensions, only the one we perceive with our senses, where there are contradictory and absurd situations that reflect perfection, as well. There are situations that somehow succeed even though we do not know how and why, and maybe they should not have succeeded, or they did so contrary to our original plan, and there are those situations that we cannot make work, no matter how hard we try. Good intentions and deeds backfire and bring very negative consequences sometimes, and tragedies and catastrophes can lead to very good results. That is why we must have awareness of the higher and unknown, to trust that it is not hostile but simply unfamiliar to us. The process of the maturing of souls in this world consists of learning tolerance, and understanding how it works although we cannot see it and we are not acquainted with it, as of yet. Religions are poor education for learning tolerance, even though they have certain elements of schooling. Everyday living with young souls is an education indeed. Mature souls learn on them. Young souls learn the basics in this world, what is what and how to develop the work ethic, and mature souls learn to put up with the mischief of young souls and teach them everything. Tolerance is the science for mature souls. But this science is by no means easy. Many mature souls were harmed in this school by the violence of the young souls. Many mature souls simply gave up at one point. Many of them are quite careful in their announcements, because some big soul, that endured unspeakable ordeal by the young souls, warned them against 'casting pearls before the swine'. Still, a lot more young souls get hurt because of their ignorance than mature souls because of their knowledge; if it were the other way round the development would go backwards. This way there is progress, albeit slow progress.

The hardest thing is to find the right measure, when a situation calls for help and when it is best not to intervene. For the older souls the most challenging experience is when they cannot prevent young souls from going through some hard and painful experience where they will hurt themselves immensely. However, the majority of young souls came to this world for that exact reason - to go through hard experiences and making bad decisions so as to be able to learn on/from them. They experience it as their 'own free will'. The biggest conflicts may occur because of that. It is a sign of great wisdom knowing when and how one may act to gain experience and avoid the negative consequences, so that something can be learnt in an easier rather than the harder way. It is a challenge for both, the young and the mature souls.

Therefore, we as souls should learn to do both – to enjoy everything, because everything is a reflection of the divine consciousness, and put up with everything, as well, because a whole is made up of both, and all the oppositions, also the ones we do not see due to the limitations of the physical body, and the ones we do not like much.

If we just enjoy and avoid the unpleasant things, we then avoid the lessons of the whole.

Very often it is a characteristic of both the young and the mature souls.

Many important bits and pieces of information and insights come to us through negative experiences. Experiences are mostly negative because we resist growing up and learning, because we do not see the whole.

The wholeness always provides us with everything we need, but our little mind is sometimes incapable of perceiving the big picture. It sees what it likes at the moment. Everything new that is unknown to us, but we need it, often comes to us in an unpleasant and violent way, or we see it as such. It appears like a tyranny of reality, and people who implement it look like tyrants to us. Still, that what conditions us, cannot be a tyrant.

It is very naive to believe that our kindred souls are just the ones we fall in love at the first sight. People we see as our enemies and tormentors may be as much our kindred souls as the former ones. It is especially so, when we are connected to those people through marriage or close family ties. We find it hard to endure them or they keep forcing us into conflicts that move the boundaries of our perception and action, but we are attached to them and there is no way out. So, they end up teaching us things we would much rather avoid, and we could never learn that on our own. They are here as tyrants only to make us go through certain experiences we would not even like to try.[19] Hence, their influence in our life we experience as tyranny. For something like that we always need help. Many great souls incarnate on purpose to play out the role of the villain because they are aware of the importance of such an act. The biggest and the most significant things can only be implemented by force. It could be said that in this world the positive and the negative influences, inspiration and coercion, carrot and stick, are all equally present.

The beginning of comprehending consciousness of the soul in this world is in cessation of identification with the body and this world. The supreme understanding of the divine consciousness is in realizing that this world is

---

[19] On the very important role of the tyrants or petty tormentors see the works of Carlos Castaneda

the divine consciousness itself, because nothing but it could ever exist. In other words, this is when people come to the point of seeing the divine consciousness in everything and everything in divine consciousness. Everything in between is the world of human happiness and misery that oscillates between resisting divine consciousness and a hasty aspiration toward it. All human suffering and joy are just a matter of speed of raising awareness of the soul in this world, a matter of consciousness of higher dimensions, a matter of perception. More accurately put: it is a question of the presence or absence of the consciousness of the soul. Sublime cognition brings balance and the understanding that everything is already perfect as it is. All the imbalance is only in the mind of man, and its reality is of the virtual kind. Therefore, the sublime cognition is just the matter of the transcendence of mind. All real spiritual traditions point to the transcendence of mind and submission to a higher consciousness. From the ecstasy of shamans, and the resurrection of Jesus, to the enlightenment of Buddha.

Buddha said that he achieved nothing new with his enlightenment, he only saw what is, that everything is perfect, and he saw his own nature as a reflection of that perfection. It means that Buddha's nature is in all of us (*bodhi*), as our essence. Enlightenment is an insight that it has always been there. That everything is alright. That life has been nothing but a lucid dream.

OUR BODY IS PERFECT
OUR ACTIONS SPOIL IT

One of the most common reasons for being frustrated with life is physical looks and health. They are rarely ideal or satisfactory. More often they are source of the greatest suffering and disappointment and we, therefore, must work on them to make them better. That, too, has its perfect reasons.

If there is a reason for everything which extends across several dimensions and many lifetimes, then it is easy to understand that our looks is no coincidence, but it is a perfect reflection of the previous causes. If we do not see the causes due to the limitations of our perception, it does not mean they do not exist, and it is pretty in vain to consider life imperfect because of it.

It is impossible to understand why we have a body like this outside the context of reincarnation and karma. If we dismiss that, we view our imperfect body as bad luck and imperfection of nature, and a nice-looking one as sheer stroke of luck. It is generally known that facial features are a giveaway of human character. The same, however, works for his entire body and medical condition. Our character did not just originate at birth, it extends across all our lives. To be able to understand why we have the body we do, it is important to say that it best reflects our character which is the consequence of our karmic maturity within the reincarnation cycle.

The shape of our body and its abilities match perfectly the intention of the soul and its plan for the current life. Soul has not only mapped its life out, but has carefully selected the body for it, as well, which will enable itself to experience life at its fullest. It has predicted everything. If experiencing personal difficulties due to working on oneself and the characteristics of the mind in the body is the topic for the life in question, then the body will be adequate for a lesson of this kind, where the mind will be afflicted with the game of cards that have been dealt. If the plan for living is to leave a mark on the outside world, the body will correlate with this intention, it will be healthy and able and it will not create any problems for the man. Therefore, if the mind is right, the body will be healthy. If there is no other way for the consciousness of the soul to correct the attitude of the mind, it will use the body to do so, because the mind is completely attached to the body. For the consciousness of the mind in the body to be made to choose the right path, meaning for the consciousness of the soul and higher understanding of reality, very often difficulties regarding health may arise. The ailment of the body is often a cure for the soul, a means of changing the paradigm of the mind in a proper way.[20]

The appearance of the body has a similar function. It is always such to facilitate the plan of life experience. If you should not experience something, you will be deprived this experience by having a very unattractive body. For example, a strong attachment to sexual expe-

---

[20] For more information on this subject see the books: The Healing Power of Illness by Thorwald Dethlefsen/Ruediger Dahlke and Disease as the Language of the Soul by Ruediger Dahlke. (Thorwald Dethlefsen/Ruediger Dahlke: Krankheit als Weg. Deutung und Be-Deutung der Krankheitsbilder; Ruediger Dahlke: Krankheit als Sprache der Seele. Be-Deutung und Chance der Krankheitsbilder)

riences will be made difficult with an undesirable body. It is a case where the obsession with sex and looks is not the prime subject the soul chose to incarnate here for, and there is a more important thing to be done in that life. One should not be depressed about that, but he/she should search for his/her true purpose in life, which is always very far away from having fun with sensual pleasures. We can always know our true purpose by ascertaining what it is that we objectively can and cannot do, not to waste time on illusions of the mind, not to adjust reality to our wishes.

On the other hand, difficulties with the body often present a challenge mind should overcome in order to develop certain characteristics. Therefore, looks and the state the body is in, are not necessarily limiting, but also stimulating since it enhances the creative endeavor and accomplishments. Practically, everything is there to stimulate us. We discover this when we discover reality.

It is also important to know that our physical looks and health are not only a result of the plan of soul for the current incarnation, but it is also a consequence of our deeds from previous (other) lives. Our body is the combination of both influences, and a reflection of our karma, past, and plans for the future development. Psychic people can see someone's karma just by looking at the body. Actually, you do not have to be particularly psychic to conclude that somebody who has an awful-looking body is burdened with bad karma. Hence, facing our bodily difficulties is one of the effective methods of correcting the mistakes we had made before. It all is our work on ourselves, it is all a process through which mind in the physical body connects to the consciousness of the soul.

Our ignorance to a large extent shapes our body. You are overweight because you do not know how to eat properly. Colon cancer and diabetes you get because of too much meat in your diet. Autism and all autoimmune diseases are side effects of the vaccines and heavy metals in them. It is all a consequence of ignorance and harmful actions, and not the imperfection of nature. There is no 'genetic error', there are only karmic consequences that leave an impact on the body. Hypnosis is the best proof for this. In hypnosis man can alter his DNA, and cure his illnesses that medicine treats as 'genetic defect' for which there is no cure. It proves that consciousness is at the base of everything that goes on in the body, and this consciousness is independent of the body, precedes and surpasses it.

From the viewpoint of consciousness that conditions living, everything has been given perfectly. The very functioning of the body reflects the divine consciousness and creativity, the body is a self-sufficient, quality mechanism that, with a little help of nature, is perfectly able to sustain itself. The only disorder may arise as a result of violence or ignorance, when the mind poisons its body out of ignorance, and causes it to fall ill.

All diseases have their common cause in toxicity, or body poisoning. If we wish to get well, we should detox, we should cleanse our metabolism from toxins. Only one disease exists, and that is the cell functioning disorder (CFD). There is only one cure: cell functioning renewal, allowing the nature to do its job. It is achieved by eating a living food that has living cells, a vegan diet, for example. However, the complete cell functioning is not something that is taught to students on universities. It is a best kept secret, maybe because the public would be made aware of the fact that a life of a single cell is as complex and intelligent as the life of a man. If cells were given the opportunity to heal, the pharmaceutical companies would go without profit. The truth is concealed.

For example, we are told that sunlight is the source of all the life on planet earth, but we are not exactly told what that means. Photons from the sun that reach the body are carriers of information that affect the functioning of the DNA directly. The light from the stars informs DNA how to work. However, 'scientists' (who work for the pharmaceutical companies) are very loud today in convincing us that sunlight is very harmful. There are more sick people today than ever before.

Apart from sunlight and fruit, the universal cure for all diseases, from flu to cancer, is 'amniotic fluid' where the fetus grows during pregnancy and feeds off it. With 'amniotic fluid' man can cure himself from even the most complicated diseases. If you are wondering where to come by 'amniotic fluid', you should know that it is your urine. The 'amniotic fluid' is urine, with some hormonal additives to help the fetus grow. All the peoples in this world in all the continents noticed that babies are born with urine, and they deduced logically that it must have healing properties. They tested it practically, and this is how urine therapy originated, the oldest and the most potent medical treatment anywhere in the world. In *Ayurveda* treatment with urine is considered the most powerful. The principle of functioning lies in the fact that urine contains all the information about the body, and by readministering urine the body gets informed and an effect similar to that of the biofeedback or homeopathic remedy is achieved, boosting the immune system over the top, and focusing on the true causes of illness. This renews the cell functioning. Urine therapy is the only real vaccination, that is prevention. However, the scientific mind has hidden away this truth from people and made them detest their own urine, because if they did not, the pharmaceutical industry would go down. Fortunately, there are more and more doctors practicing urine therapy today, they organize their congresses on a global scale and exchange results and experiences.

In the modern world, disease is used to gain profit because the pharmaceutical industry is in complete control of the allopathic medicine and education. Only the symptoms get treated, not the causes of illnesses. Instead of curing and healing, all the allopathic 'remedies' are antibiotics, steroids (synthetic hormones) and analgetics, and they all fall under the category of immunosuppressive medications, that is agents aimed at killing life (anti – bios). Their logic is simple: they eliminate the life of cells causing the life of the body to be eliminated so as to eliminate the disease, the pathogens that cause it, but our organism is bigger and stronger and it will survive, and tumor and pathogens are smaller and they will die first. This is, in a nutshell, the 'logics' of modern medicine, more precisely the pharmaceutical industry: a controlled and systematic killing of the body in order to kill the disease.

A true cause and a successful method in cancer treatment was discovered by Otto Heinrich Warburg back in 1923. for which he received the Nobel prize. The cause of cancerogenic tumors isan increased acidity of the organism, and the treatment is, apart from detox, a change of diet that enhances the alkalinity of the body (vegan diet, active oxygen, sodium ascorbate). The secret is in the right pH value of the organism. However, in those days, the pharmaceutical industry was on the rise, as part of the petroleum industry, and before long the greed for profit prevailed, the truth was put aside and chemotherapy, which maximally increases the acidity of the organism, was introduced. It systematically kills the organism, but brings huge profits.

In the Middle Ages crooks were selling 'magic potions' in town squares for all the existing diseases. Nowadays crooks sell vaccines as 'magic potions' for the diseases-to-be. The already existing income they regularly receive from the sick people is not enough, they had to go out and convince the public that healthy children and people need their heavy poison cocktail (severe toxins are ingredients of every vaccine) to protect themselves from future diseases. They make money off healthy people. By doing so they turn all the healthy people into their clients, into patients. Never throughout the entire history of human kind have the children been so sick like they are today. Statistics show and prove that vaccinated children are ten times more sick than unvaccinated ones.

How can this be explained by the perfection of the world we are describing here? The answer is quite simple: everything is perfect, human ignorance, deception and stupidity, as well. All the negative phenomena, anomalies and destructions can also be perfect. It is so because perfection is based on causality and the freedom to be whatever somebody wishes to be. Bad outcome is the consequence of a bad cause, the consequence of indulging in sloth and irresponsibility and the need to avoid creating good causes. It is not only that a handsome and healthy man is picture perfect. Murderers and insane people can also be perfect at what they do, they can have their perfectly functioning institutions. The perfection of nature does not have morality, it always and in everything follows the causality and freedom that conditions everything. However, the causality of human deeds is closely tied to the human mind. That is the only place where the problem with the bad consequences may occur, and not in nature.

There is no illness that may originate from the mal-functioning of the body or nature. The entire organism is naturally designed to be self-maintaining and self-healing. This self-preservation is what constitutes life itself. Every cell does the same. All diseases are caused by a sudden violent attack on the body's harmony and the functioning of nature. However, we have been convinced that we are imperfect and as such are unfit to live and be healthy without the 'drugs' of pharmaceutical companies. There is not a single pharmaceutical 'cure' that does not damage the organism.

One fact is evident – 90% of medical interventions are not because of some organic ailment,but because of the functional disorder people did unto themselves as a direct result of ignorance. Such functional disorders disappear all by themselves in 3 to 7 days in 99% of all cases, or can easily be removed with some traditional healing methods. Only 10% of cases have organic ailment and they in 90% of cases are a result of the very harmful effect of the prescribed medications ingested by a person who went to doctors for help because of some functional disorder.

The process of disruption of the body's perfect functioning can be explained by the following. Organism keeps healing itself constantly. It always secretes toxic matter and pathogens we have, out of ignorance or otherwise, accumulated. Secretion is normally done through the liver and colon. When the process of elimination is somewhat more complex, the organism switches to an overload mode, which manifests in the form of high temperature and virus reproduction whose sole purpose is to cleanse the body of all the pathogenic organisms. Allopathic medicine that deals with the symptoms only, has taught us that higher temperature means disease, that the cause of an illness is in the viruses, afterward we go to a doctor who prescribes a 'medication' against high temperature and it is suppressed, the healing of the entire organism has been aborted. The organism makes a go for what it can, and then it starts to solve the problem with excess secretion, diarrhea and vomiting. However, that also gets treated like a disease ('some virus') and we take another 'medication' and stop the excess secretion. Sometimes the organism tries to redirect the problems outward on the skin. We get a rash, boils on the skin and other symptoms, which we once again treat like a disease and fix using 'cures'. Or the organism tries to secrete through the lungs and we cough and secrete. This, too, is stopped with 'cures' for the cough, that simply paralyze this process and we think we have been cured. When the organism fails yet again to get rid of the toxic matter from within, it is forced to make containers or mini bags in which to isolate and dispose of the unwanted matter. Those are tumors. That is why an average organism is full of tumors of various shapes and sizes. When toxins hit through the roof and 'healing' of this kind begins to put spikes in the wheel of the real self-healing of organism, cancer is the next step, tumors become cancerogenic, pathogenic, they start to spread all over the body uncontrollably. The other alternative is the vital organs are no longer capable of protecting themselves and they begin to shut down. It is a closed circle which grosses super profits for the pharmaceutical industry at the expense of people.

The best medicine in the world cannot cure the man who spent a bigger part of his life poisoning his own metabolism with inadequate lifestyle and diet. This is the reason why before any treatment a thorough cleansing of the organism is required. The cleansing of the organism is healing in itself. It is best performed with the raw food only, based on raw fruit and vegetables. Anatomically, the human body is neither that of a meat-eater, nor a plant-eater, but a fruit-eater.

Likewise, the most powerful method of healing and rejuvenating the body is intermittent fasting. During fasting the body gets completely renewed and cleansed, there is a serious increase in stem cell count in the organism.

The importance of health in the perfection of nature is clear from the issue of viruses and bacteria, which is yet another deception of science. All diseases are intoxication of the organism induced by bacteria. Bacteria are the laborers that transmute and develop all biological life. The basis of the biological life is a cell. The cells of all the living beings were bacteria once that merged in symbiosis to make the bodies of plants and animals. Since bacteria serve all life forms, their merging is inevitable, some are found where they should not be found, and do what they should not do on that spot. To prevent these situations from happening, the immune system exists in every living being to regulate the functioning of bacteria, and by doing so the functioning of the organism itself. The immune system regulates the overall situation in various ways, sometimes using the bacteria it needs, and sometimes by reproducing the viruses whose purpose is to regulate the life of bacteria. The body uses the viruses to defend itself against the harmful bacteria that found themselves where they do not belong. Viruses are the means of body cleansing, nothing else, like soap. *Viruses originate in the body for the purpose of healing. Any different functioning of the viruses is the consequence of artificial intervention and manipulation on them in the form of biological weapon*. Unlike bacteria viruses are not living beings, they do not have metabolism. Because they are of the body and intended for the body, they cannot live outside of the body. They can survive outside the body from several minutes to four days, depending on the conditions. For the same reason they cannot survive in the body of another species.

While the body reproduces the viruses for internal cleansing, externally the same effect is achieved against harmful bacteria by simply maintaining hygiene. All viruses have a special purpose, but they, too, can be found where they do not belong, and cause the counter effect. The same way eating some detergent is not healthy, viruses can be dangerous if they are found in some body they were not originally intended for, which has no specific need for them. All big diseases were started from bacteria (and parasites) and lack of hygiene. It happens to people individually, and on a large scale as epidemics following the same pattern. All great epidemics were eradicated by the improved hygienic standards and the living conditions of people. Never with vaccination. No great epidemics ever broke out naturally, but always in an artificial way, through human intervention, or more precisely through the intervention of those who manipulate with people[21] The nature always eliminated the epidemics.

Hence, the issue of health cannot in any way corrupt the perfection of existence. If we have been given life itself, it is logical that it was given to us in a way it can sustain itself. A useful piece of advice is not to poison it but to let it heal. The only problem is in our mind, more

[21] For more details on who, how and why manipulates people, see my book 'The Fantastic History of Galaxy, Earth and Human Species'.

accurately in our handling of our own body. The problem has never been about the body, at all. If we do not see the causes of some disorder in the functioning of the body in the current life, they might as well be in the previous one, in karma.

Indeed, the biggest part of what we attribute to imperfection of life is actually based on our ignorance and refusal to accept responsibility for what we do, and the things we do not do, but should. We do not only face the consequences of our activities, but also of our inactivity. Everything we omit to do, but should have done, the perfection of nature will make us pay the price for. If it were not like that, nature would not be perfect. It is all for our own good.

To put it simply, the state of the body cannot be properly understood if we observe it from the same, material level, from the level of the body itself. We must have insight into the higher levels of existence, into the karmic causes. If we observe the body as only a sensory and bodily phenomenon, everything negative that happens to it looks like a series of mistakes and unfortunate circumstances, the consequence of imperfection.

With the body, much like with everything else, the true insight we can attain only by rising above the bodily and material limitations. The more we rise, the clearer it becomes that everything is perfect. The more limited we are in our perception, the more everything appears as imperfect.

CAUSALITY AND FREE WILL
ARE CONNECTED PERFECTLY

There is a false dilemma whether the world is ruled by coincidence or predetermination, freedom or causality. This false dilemma is imposed by forces that keep people in the state of ignorance, and those are the forces that rule over the highest education and science. What lurks behind this question is actually the attitude that advocates coincidence as a smoke screen for the materialism of science, and the attitude of predetermination calls for religious acceptance of god's will and promoting the attitude of church. They both keep us in the dark by concealing the true role of the soul in this world.

In reality what really rules the world is freedom and causality. They are not conflicted but complementary.

Freedom conditions all the changes and creativity, whereas causality gives stability and continuity to everything. If everything were free and coincidental, the world would be a chaos. If everything were predetermined, cosmos would be an unconscious machine without creativity and change, everything would be conditioned and predictable, no consciousness would be required.

Upon taking a closer look we can see that unity of freedom and causality happens in a more complex way.

Causality may stem from:

1. Us. We create the causes with our own deeds, our karmic maturity and our state of consciousness, we attract certain events and beings to implement them.

2. The outside world, other beings and their karma, as well as the mental patterns which attract events that will affect us, because we happen to be in the zone of their influence.

3. The nature and non-organic beings. Influences over events that nature implements are planetary, explained in great detail by the science of astrology, which is based on the holographic model of cosmos, proving that everything is interconnected in one whole, whereas space and time are relative. The influence of non-organic beings are influences from the astral world, conscious energy entities that are not of this world. These influences are extremely rare, but they can happen.

All three types of causality may be connected and synchronized. Our mental frame which is determined by our karmic maturity acts as the chief attractor of events, where everything is coordinated with the planetary influences and assisted by nature and other beings as mediators and aides that help to realize the goal.

There is the fourth principle of phenomena taking place that encompasses the first three. It is the principle of self-realization. Everything happens only because of it. The Absolute itself manifests in the form of universe for the sake of awareness of all the possibilities. This principle regarding the nature of phenomena is as follows: *to the measure we move toward the self-knowing of our soul, the consciousness of existence, we manage to overcome all the manifestations. The only way out of the causality which conditions, of the tyranny of coincidence, is the path of self-knowing, the awareness and awakening.*

Therefore, we are conditioned in all the possible ways, but in such a manner which offers only one way out to freedom: self-knowledge of the unconditioned consciousness that conditions everything. It is perfectly logical. If we try to do anything else, we are conditioned then, we face the forces of nature that do this, not us. We attribute some deeds to ourselves because we live in an illusion. Nature does it all, because as we have stated before, the potential for all the deeds and phenomena already exists in nature in its unmanifested, quantum state. There is nothing new in nature. What was unmanifested becomes manifested, any manifestation in our immediate surroundings is initiated by the consciousness of our mind, and then we attribute it to ourselves, as though it was us who did it. We rejoice or suffer because of it. We have never done anything, our soul is always the witness of events, only our mind assigned all the deeds to itself. The only thing we can actually do, for which we have been granted freedom, is the act of moving toward freedom, toward the transcendence of the natural causality, a turning to the transcendental consciousness of the divine soul. It was so wisely set up that we do not have the slightest chance of escaping ourselves, the only thing we can really do is get to know ourselves. For that reason, everything else is an illusion. That is the only freedom we have in the overall existence. The price of that freedom is unobtrusiveness. This freedom we must choose alone and use it as the landmark on our life path. Nothing will make us go down that road like the awareness of the fact that all other roads lead to nowhere. It is the least-traveled road. In esoteric teachings it is described as a narrow path that leads to life, as opposed to wide roads paved with good intentions and desires that lead to hell and death.

There are events and deeds we need for personal growth and which we preplanned during the course of this life or even before it. There are deeds we never signed up for, but we put up with them because we happen to be in the zone of their influence, we live in a densely populated world and we have an effect on one another in a planned, but also in an unplanned way.

However, even such unplanned and accidental events contribute to the creativity of our consciousness through the challenge and risk. If it were not for them, we would live our life cut off from any possibility of growth or change. If an unplanned event causes difficulty or suffering, it may be an indication that we have become too laid back in our comfort zone. The larger part of suffering refers to the resistance of our mind/ego and its need to avoid change, growth and development. ***Restrictions, coercions and constraints we are exposed to in this world, are the most important methods of our growth and awakening***. They are a part of the conscious intention which is at the base of existence. Due to our unconsciousness we need to be corrected and guided from the outside world when we make a mistake, because we are not always capable of going in the right direction of our own free will. We often forget that consciousness is at the base of all existence then when something is not to our liking or when we get hurt. It is a characteristic of young souls. Mature souls are aware of the fact that the consciousness of existence is at the same time their own consciousness, because there are not several consciousnesses that govern existence. Any type of conflict with the facts of reality, any imbalance and adversity, mature souls recognize as their own mistake and a challenge leading to the awareness, not as a mistake of reality, or the non-existence of consciousness at the base of everything.

The younger the soul is and the more immature, the more its understanding is limited to the sensory perception, the more it sees the world as an imperfect series of material coincidences. For that reason it keeps tying itself to the conflict with the world more and more. Hence, it aspires more toward the comfort and safety. The principle of pleasure is its benchmark. Besides, anyone could see that people whose sole life goal is personal fortune and comfort are the most stupid, superficial and hypocritical individuals. Pleasure may present a challenge for the man that diverts him from the right and good in his life, the same way it is a proof of knowledge and appropriateness. Trouble and distress may pose a challenge for the man to find the right path, to come to his senses, as much as they can be a result of unconsciousness and mistakes. That is the true meaning of spare the rod and spoil the child.

The more mature the soul is, the more it is aware of its limitations, that what it cannot see at the moment also exists, it recognizes and appreciates the consciousness of the very existence, the causes that surpass the body and one life. It has more and more come to terms with the world. The most mature soul is in ecstasy of the conscious unity with existence. It has ended its karmic cycle.

Naturally, there are difficulties and suffering that do not seem justified, that destroy careers and lives and the circumstances do not appear to come from the person in question. Such difficulties are the hardest to accept as part of existence. However, they are only seemingly unjustified because their cause is not in one life only. Every suffering that appears as unjustified has its cause we do not see, which is part of the plan of multiple lives and karmic cycles. Its reason may be in historical epoch or the collective program of a nation an individual takes part in.

Everything has its time, civilizations rise and fall, peoples develop and deform, life is somewhere simple and easy, and somewhere hard and complicated. When the whole nation goes down, the individuals go down, as well. Examples of such lives where the suffering seems undeserved we have in primitive parts of the world where there is famine, and people die as a result of the poor quality of life. The reason for this lies in karmic immaturity. Very young souls find it hard to cope with this world. Although they have natural resources at their disposal they do not know how to work and create. Short and hard life must be viewed in the wider context, that of the karma and incarnations. The causes of such a life are not visible from the perspective of that one life. Young souls in their initial stages of incarnations live very short lives, gradually adjusting to the life on the physical plane. Death of a child in Africa seen from a higher perspective, from the point of karmic maturing, is no tragedy, but a perfectly logical chain of events. It is also a logical chain of events that the mature souls help them to survive, and as much as possible learn something while they are still in this world. By doing so, the mature souls help to make planet earth a better place to live.

The unity of freedom and causality reflects itself on all the spheres of life and existence. In our experience we see them in the relationship of the soul and the body, of being born and dying. Body is the result of the causality of this world, of the space and time more than anything, which like a hologram imprints the predetermination of the movements of the body, its destiny. The science of astrology, which is based entirely on the holographic principles of universe, shows this perfectly.

Consciousness of the soul is transcendental and merges with the physical body causing the dialectics of their relationship. At times, one prevails, and at other times, the other one does. Body has its consciousness, personified in the mind. The body receives this consciousness from the consciousness of the soul, of course, but it was given to it to use as its consciousness. The dialectics of the body and soul creates all the human drama and karma in this world. The simplest way of experiencing it in ourselves is in the form of a conflict between instincts and awareness, the lower and the higher nature, free will and coercion, mechanicalness in our habits and the need to change, discrepancy between material and spiritual. In reality, in every relationship between coercion and free will. Often it is quite clear the way it is, as a relationship between the soul and the body.

The relationship between the soul and the body would require a lot more writing space. Although, it has already been described in all the novels, dramas and poetry. It is the life story of any man. It is the history of humankind. We can briefly reminisce about some of their hidden phenomena that will shed some light on this topic, and that is the perfection of all the phenomena and existence itself.

The soul gives us all the freedom of trying out all the options, and the body gives us all the limitations of this process. At the point of their pressure and friction, consciousness is crystallized in this world. We all battle the difficulties of the physical world and mature during this process. Body acts like a brake to the instant and timeless consciousness of existence, the body slows the consciousness down in order for the consciousness to be able to encompass all the details. Consciousness of the soul gives all the life and meaning of existence to the world. Besides, we are only too familiar with the scenario of what happens to the body when the consciousness of the soul abandons it. It stinks up and rots. If you ever took a closer look at the corpse, you would have to feel indifferent toward it, when you see the emptiness of it, when you see there is nothing there. The corpse frightens us, its emptiness without a soul because we are only used to seeing the soul in the body.

The basis characteristic of the effect the soul has on the body is unobtrusiveness. It merely inspires and attracts so that the smaller part of its consciousness which is in the body could recognize its real nature, its soul. The soul would achieve nothing if it forced itself on people. The essence of the drama of life is for the consciousness of the soul to be able to recognize itself in the body, for this consciousness to be maintained and kept in all the possible states of the body and mind, so one can never lose it and forget in existence. Then it is recognized as the essence of the very existence, and existence to be recognized as the divine consciousness.

Causality and free will cross paths the most and their discrepancies are best resolved through the work of man. When we said that restrictions, coercions and constraints we are exposed to in this world, are the most important methods of our growth and awakening, it mostly referred to work and the conditions of work.

Work is the type of coercion the consciousness of the soul faces in the reality of the physical world. Through work it learns of reality and manifests its abilities and creativity. Work makes the man, on the other hand, man using his work, makes the world around himself. However, to most people work is plight and torture. There are two reasons for that. The first one refers to the historical context. Work during the Middle Ages was much harder than it is today. In the future it will be much easier than today. Therefore, there is no use in complaining, instead let us make it that way. The second reason is individual karmic maturity of the soul. Young and immature souls have yet to get acquainted with the working conditions on the physical plane, they are taking baby steps first. That is why everything seems so hard for them. But it is not work itself that is hard, but their immaturity.

With work we create new circumstances and new conditions the nature had not anticipated and cannot create all by itself. It benefits the creativity of the consciousness of the soul, it brings new challenge for us. Indeed, man has no bigger challenge in this world than the consequences of his actions.

Work as the type of coercion breaks the inertia of the soul, its overly attractive power that makes people inert and complacent. Without work man degenerates. All those who in a flash destroyed their own and other people's lives had too much free time on their hands, and means, money they did not earn. At best, such cases become complacent sloths, negative to themselves. Look into your heart and be true to yourself – what would you do if you did not have to get up early in the morning and go to work? Come up with the worst case scenario and you will be just about right.

There is a simple truth behind all this, the lower mind always aspires to go downward, to the line of the least resistance, to an ever bigger self-indulgence and letting go. It has a program within to experience absolutely everything it can experience. This freedom is a condition for creativity, but until it reaches that point of creativity it is the source of all the problems. That is why it needs work, order and discipline, as well as, all the power of legislative, executive and judicial authority.

Only very few people are able to bring together work and pleasure, to do what they are talented for, and what they love. Majority of people cannot do this, so they have to be forced. However, there is no need for everyone to be creative and talented, for normal living simple workers will do, who will produce food and other necessities. Observed from the perspective of the Whole we all belong to, their hard work is just as valuable, although at first glance it does not appear so; without them creative people could not do anything.

Coercion and enforcement must exist in ourlives, for the consciousness of the soul to express itself properly and adjust to this world. Faced with the challenges of this world the consciousness of the soul begins to awaken. The world is designed in such a way. Such is the nature of consciousness. Consciousness is like existence itself which exists always, but how? Only its expression matters, not existence itself. Coercions, restrictions and difficulties must exist in order to be overcome, and in doing so, the consciousness of the soul gets crystallized. All of it has a perfectly positive role. Man learns the most once he is forced to turn to the unknown, to do things he does not want to, when he is faced with new challenges. Always when he moves within the familiar boundaries and on the field he organized to fit his needs, he stops growing.

Facing the unknown would come a lot easier if he became aware of the fact that this wider unfamiliar whole that oppresses him so, is just as aware as he is, that it is the same divine consciousness, within and without, and therefore nothing can be negative. When he accepts the whole in such a way, everything seems positive, so much so that the existing difficulties begin to fade.

For as long as man experiences the outer world as alien and unconscious nature, it will be the proof that he, too, is unconscious. Man cannot be truly conscious in any other way except by recognizing the entire existence as conscious.

Up until that point all the coercions and constraints are the lesser evil than allowing an unconscious man to do as he likes. The wholeness sees this clearly, and therefore, it does not permit so. However, he experiences that as suffering.

Man comes by this knowledge the harder way, when the worst torment forces him to make the biggest sacrifice, to unravel the best in him, to express the consciousness of his soul then when it is the hardest.

It all takes place due to the dialectics of opposites which depicts the overall existence adding a touch of charm to its every detail.

THE PERFECTION MANIFESTS ITSELF
THROUGH THE DIALECTICS OF OPPOSITIONS

The perfection of divine Absolute manifests itself currently or timelessly in one way only, as its exact opposite in the form of the 'divine particle', which also currently, vibrating according to the model of golden section, keeps forming an ever more complex shapes of existence, all the cosmos and life. This primary opposition according to the model of hologram reflects and mirrors itself in everything else that exists. The truth is that everything exists as a reflection of this primary opposition. This opposition is dialectical, it does not suppress itself, because it does not repeat itself mechanically, there is nothing that is identical in existence, everything keeps developing in order to experience all the possible states. The dialectics here, like in philosophy, means the unity of opposition, the testing of oppositions in order to surpass them, to reach transcendence and the correct understanding of the whole or the essence of things. It is a way in which intellect gains insight into matter.

Trying out all the opposites for the purpose of awareness in the physical body we feel directly for all our life, and in all our lives. We keep on incarnating until the point we attain the primordial unity beyond all oppositions, until we are able to transcend the opposites in the awareness of unison. We come to this world just to be crucified on the cross of all the oppositions, and having gone through them personally, we manage to surpass them and reach the divine consciousness of unity. More accurately, to go back to it, because nothing happens outside of it.

Understanding that the perfection of the whole becomes manifested through the oppositions brings us closer to the goal of this book.

The experience of opposition in this world is the subject of almost all the other spiritual teachings. They usually differentiate an absolute or an authentic state, which is associated with the divine or real, and the state which is not absolute but relative, changeable and conditioned, the state of painful experiences of all the oppositions, of being born and reborn. The ultimate goal of human life and all the spiritual efforts boils down to the knowledge of the absolute nature of existence and surpassing the relative one, the overcoming of oppositions by knowing the unity.

Understanding will not remove suffering with a magic wand, but it will remove it surely over a period of years, because we live here in time, conditioned by the physical laws that have their processes and cannot be instantly suppressed or changed. Mind is both out of time and in time, and this different rhythm keeps confusing people, they find it hard to grasp mentally that what they think cannot be manifested instantly on the physical plane. All thoughts get realized, thoughts are ideas for shaping the reality into all the possible forms, ideas which manifest all the possibilities, but on the physical plane the laws of causality in linear time rule, which makes it hard for thoughts to be realized instantly. All the human work and science serve to adjust timeless thoughts and ideas with the physical reality in time. Once we completely adjust one idea to the physical reality in linear time, we have materialized this idea. *The time distance between an idea and its physical manifestation exists for the idea and the entire process of its realization to be completely understood, in all the aspects. This time distance is pro-*

duced by the different dimensions an idea goes through on its way to materialrealization. Different dimensions exist so that the full spectrum of the possibilities of existence could be manifested. Slowness and inertia of the physical world enable the awareness of all the possibilities of action. Although from the perspective of the higher consciousness inertia of the physical world appears limiting and negative, it is not. Slowness and inertia of the physical world enable seeing and experiencing every phenomenon in all its aspects and possibilities.

Therefore, every form of understanding, even a partial one, returns us to the unity with the perfection of existence. Understanding is the only cure for all diseases and all the suffering of human existence. All types of conflicts that happen between people have their in common origin in the lack of understanding, and they can all be resolved by understanding, although not all at once. If we could rise above the body and go to higher dimensions, something we can achieve with the practice of meditation, we would see that we are all parts of the same tree of life, leaves on the same branch, that our quarrel and conflict belong to the rougher and more stupid versions of experiences of all the potentials of existence.

Understanding that is in our focus here is actually our ability to understand how the Absolute keeps manifesting itself: through the oppositions. Therefore, all the oppositions we experience and see are no proof that existence is not perfect, on the contrary. The perfection of existence is there all the time, but we fail to see it in its entirety, in all the dimensions and proportions of existence, we see a tiny fragment in space and time, and it appears logical to us that this piece, separated from the whole, seems imperfect, insufficient, transient, even negative and evil. *Oppositions are a way in which the perfection of existence keeps manifesting, they are not the proof that everything is not perfect.* However, the nature of our experiences is such that the whole context and the meaning of events are full of oppositions we can see only from the higher dimensions, which contain everything we already have here but look separated in space and time of the physical world, which once again gets merged and compressed into one conscious and meaningful whole. People who fall short of the systematic spiritual practice of awareness, are able to access those higher dimensions only after the death of the physical body. The same can be achieved during the physical life in the body by means of spiritual practice, meditation, and with out-of-body experiences.

There are objective and real oppositions, which relate to the natural laws, to the space and time we reside in. They cannot be avoided or changed, but they can be comprehended.

There are the subjective ones, as well, the ones that only seemingly appear to be oppositions, because we do not see the whole, we cannot see the dimensions through which the processes unravel and the meaning of events, the whole in its entirety. They are the hardest to recognize and comprehend.

Subjective or ostensible oppositions we experience most often due to the vagueness of some process of karmic experiences we happen to be going through. Each incarnation has its subject matter to be resolved, something that man is meant to experience during the course of the current life. Often there are more than one topics to deal with. However, it is invariably the case where one theme of life cannot be experienced during a single incarnation, which makes the drama extend across several acts, that is several lives. Since from our current perspective in this life we are aware of the events of this life only, it causes commotion. What we experience in one life may seem without closure and illogical, meaningless and evil. However, it is only one chapter in the book of life that extends across a large number of physical births.

There are subjects where one life is plenty. The person then experiences extreme oppositions in that one life, both failure and success, he experiences one to become aware of the other. In such a way, he strengthens his consciousness and creativity, which is the true intention of soul in this world.

Some subjects require two lives. Usually, those are the subjects that refer to the experience of the perpetrator and his/her victim. Classical explanation of karma is that if we committed some evil deed or violence in the previous life, in this life we will fall victim to a similar crime in order to experience and maybe 'redeem' ourselves, 'to pay off our karmic debt' and grow in awareness. This is a typical action-reaction interpretation of karma. It may be true for some karmic issues, but not for all. Life is too complex and expensive to be squandered on only one type of experiences. It is usually used maximally for everything that can be used.

For an action-reaction situations two lives are usually enough, because it is questionable whether somebody can transform from the mental pattern of bully to penitent. There are such cases, but too few to mention. Restarting to a new life is usually necessary, and the change of the physical mind together with the body so that the opposite state can be experienced.

There are those subjects that require more than two lives. They are more complex than the simple action-reaction experiences. That is why they are harder for recognizing and understanding the oppositions that happen to us in the current life of ours. Besides, only the level of maturity of an individual consciousness decides whether some topic will extend across several lives or we will become aware of it in only one life. The most complex and complicated topic can be resolved within the space of only one lifetime, there are no obstacles in the way, but there are too few mature souls that can pull it off. Such a life is also very expensive. Too much has been invested in it and all the experiences are more intense, especially the suffering. Usually such an incarnation is the last one in the incarnation cycle of one soul, before its final liberation from the cycle of being-born-and-dying, which denotes the self-knowledge of the soul. Namely, the need for new incarnations ceases when one soul becomes aware of itself to such a degree that it is able to recognize the unity of all the oppositions it experiences in this world, and this unity can be known only in the light of the divine consciousness which conditions everything, which the soul itself is.

Apart from all that, one should know that there are topics and experiences where one person is simply not enough. A few souls join in, many have supporting roles but important in some way, some are just extras. It will be very hard for them to understand the meaning of their lives, because that meaning will, to a minute degree, be related to them. They are largely in service of somebody else, they are part of a bigger game. The biggest number of souls in this world have roles like that, they are mostly young souls who learn the game by watching from the perspective of a sideshow, to become bigger players, to mature. For bigger roles more maturity is required and experience.

Some souls that are trying to sort out their lives may walk in our life and disrupt it unintentionally. There is too much traffic in this world. This world is a scene for playing out a large number of simultaneous dramas. This world is a multidimensional holographic theater. However, it may happen that overlapping and bumps take place, unplanned things. It does not mean that in the long run everything is not perfect as is. Such cases are all part of the perfection because they add freedom to such events increasing the need for the creativity of souls. If everything were ideally staged, it would be boring, the game would not make much sense. The element of freedom and unpredictability is what gives the game of life its delicious savor, and the biggest challenge to the consciousness of the soul is to express itself always in a new and a creative way. Souls have a need for such uncertainty, for the risk, it fires up the greatest passion and creativity in the game. When nothing happens they cause a quake just to move things and for something new to happen.

Likewise, there are topics that require a group of souls to act together in order for the themes of collective significance to be realized. Those are all the mass movements and historical events where the tribes and nations are involved in. Those topics cover the entire historical era or epoch. It should come as no surprise to us if a life goes by in a brief and chaotic manner, if you die in an angry mob stampede or a bomb blows you up. The question of the meaning of opposition is redundant under such circumstances. Most often we do not have the time or conditions for philosophy then. In such lives we are a ball the oppositions play a game of tennis with. Only when we are a highly developed soul can we play tennis with the oppositions. To be a player and not an instrument of the game is a big thing and only very developed souls can pull it off.

THE DIALECTICS OF LIFE AND DEATH

The first and the most general opposition we are exposed to is our birth and dying in the body. Due to the difference in the nature of the higher dimensions and the fact that there is no time in them, and the nature of the physical existence in time, it appears to us that we started to exist with the birth of the physical body. Quite the reverse. With the birth of the body we experience the planned oblivion of ourselves and our true nature, our essence or soul. With the birth we cease to exist regarding the absolute reality and fall asleep and start dreaming that we are separate from the whole of the divine Absolute.

Paradox and the dialectics of oppositions is best reflected in the very reason for our birth when we experience the oblivion of our true nature, our soul. If we were born in the body fully aware of our soul, of our past lives, we would use the already acquired wealth of experience in solving the problems and challenges of life, and the drama of life could not play out in a way where it would inspire the creativity of consciousness. It must develop in a way that it all seems like our first time, like we have never experienced it before. That is the only way for the consciousness in the body to be able to participate in life with all its passion and creativity. Otherwise it would cheat in the game or it would flee at the slightest hint of challenge, whereas what is truly required here are challenges, even the ones of the cruelest nature, because as we have stated before, here we get to experience everything we possibly can because the consciousness of the divine becomes manifested as everything that could possibly be. Opposition is, therefore, in the fact that oblivion exists for the consciousness to be generated, together with all the creativity of consciousness. Abstract consciousness manifests itself concretely through existence. All we ever do in our lives is nothing but trying out oblivion for the sake of memory, unconsciousness for the sake of awakening, mistakes to finally learn what is right.

That is why this world is not heaven, although it could be, that is why our life is imperfect and painful although it could be enlightened and perfect. We are here to experience all the oppositions of perfection because that is the only way for the full consciousness of perfection in all its possibilities to be actualized.

When our own existence we view as upside down, everything else must be upside down because our perspective is wrong.

When we experience ourselves as individuals separated from the whole, everything else we experience as being separated from the whole. Every time we recognize wholeness and unity we feel blissful and experience something like finding unity with our true self, to which we tend to assign the most supreme religious quality, although it is completely unnecessary; this is our original state. At the base of every feeling of love and mercy, goodness and understanding lies our ability to recognize the initial unity and the perfection of everything. It is what attracts us the most, primordial unity is our biggest motive in life and the chief attractor.

We reach this primordial unity through the experience of conflict and separation.

Every time we become aware of what is right in this world we do so because we experience the wrong.

Due to the freedom which allows for the manifestation of everything that can manifest and happen, our deaths range from being preplanned to being completely unplanned. Soul does not go through the planned experiences only, to a much higher degree it participates in the freedom that keeps all options open. The freedom of experiencing completely unforeseen events is what strengthens the consciousness and the will of soul in this world, and that is what finally awakens the ultimate consciousness of oneself. That is an explanation why people find risk so inviting. Creative people experience risk as a part of passion for change and creation, the less creative ones enjoy the adrenaline rush. Risk has always been an integral part of creativity and prerequisite for freedom. The influences and plans of other souls are also present and they interweave with us, not only for support and incentive, but for conflict, as well. Conflicts are also part of the creativity of consciousness, they only get expressed in a rougher way.

Consciousness which is at the base of the overall existence attracts us in a variety of ways. Young and immature souls are attracted to it in an immature way, and the mature souls in a mature way. It is simple enough, and acts like a mirror. Existence is the mirror of divine consciousness. The attraction of divine consciousness is manifested as the ecstasy of feeling accomplished and finding one's true roots. For this reason young and immature souls can find their ecstasy upon accomplishments in the most stupid things, even crime, sadism and masochism. That is the ecstasy which happens only when we experience existence as overly intensive, in extreme states, that border with death. All the limitations of the mind are removed then and consciousness which is at the base of the overall existence can finally come to the fore, and man can experience it directly in ecstasy and the feeling of fulfillment. Albeit, only for a short time and spontaneously. This happens because consciousness is at the base of existence, it is experienced in the same way during orgasm and samadhi, in deep meditation and self-knowledge. The only difference is in the maturity of approach and how long the knowing lasts, together with its application. Mature souls experience consciousness which is at the base of the overall existence in a creative and constructive way, as a part of their own growing, their own actions and existence. The immature ones are just attracted so they blindly crash into it.

Souls plan the death of this body in all kinds of ways, often through disease, accident or murder. To a lesser degree souls let their body get old and live on till the end of its possibilities. More than anything, because old age is negative in every respect, together with the negative effect it has on the consciousness in the body, and is the sum of all the difficulties that yield no results. It will suffer the ripe old age only if it is of help to a fellow soul (person). Then it will try to stay on for as long as necessary. Likewise, if they are meant to bring negative intervention in the form of coercion and pressure, all the foul experiences this other person needs to go through. Every life depends on plan and purpose. It can stay in its old age if it learns to enjoy life in the proper way, and if the body is healthy enough. Such old age is the best, the consciousness of the soul radiates from such old people. The only ugly and negative old age is the one where man has lost his bond with the soul. If he has managed to keep it and increase it, this person, then, becomes younger over time on the inside, more beautiful and interesting, there is an aura of serenity about him, nobility, purity and goodness. Others do not feel him old, only pleasant and they seek the company of such distinguished people.

If a violent death was a part of the initial plan, then there should not be a problem for the soul in its further development, in planning the remainder of its life/incarnations. The development will continue like it otherwise would, if some other circumstances were in question. Every planned death is peaceful. Man who has lived a full life dies peacefully. He knows where he is going, because he has got to know the nature of existence well. Anyone who has raised the level of awareness about the nature of reality in this world awaits the other world with glee, because he sees that there is no difference, it is all one big life and the only thing that exists is existence itself. There is no such thing as the non-existence. The only one who really suffers is the one who does not see reality for what it is.

If the violent death was unplanned, there are a number of problems a soul faces. It is interrupted during the process of gaining experiences. It has been kicked out of the body but it is still attached to the strong program of its karma for the current life. Body no longer exists, but the program still has energy and a need for closure. This leads to confusion, as well as the intention to quickly make up for the lost time and continue with the ongoing program. Such souls reincarnate quickly, often in the same space and time where the previous life was inter-rupted.

A vindictive reaction by the soul violently evicted from the body may follow suit. Many murderers testify to their newly acquired experience of not being able to sleep at night or continue to live their life, or being haunted by the ones they killed. It can go so far as to receive assis-tance by the dead victim resolving its own murder case, and finding out who done it. They do not do this so much because of themselves, but because they do not wish the crime to be repeated. Additionally, they help the perpetrator recognize his true nature and his actions, and find a way to get out of this negative state faster. Some criminals even admitted the killing after being made to do so by the dead.

An unplanned death, especially if it were a result of murder rather than natural causes, faces the soul with the issue of violence. If it were not previously involved in an experience of this case, violence or murder, it may seem shocking to it but not only from the perspective we are accustomed to here, where we project experiences in a subject-object relationship, where we directly go through our batch of experiences with the bad lot alone, and other people's we hear of, we learn indirectly and partially. When the soul is out of the body it has a much higher consciousness than while it still is in the body, the type of awareness which is comprehensive, it possesses empathy which is beyond imagination to us here. Souls that are out of the body experience other people's states of consciousness and feelings like their own. They feel everything the other people experienced when something was done to them. The experience of the killer who killed the victim's body as a result of his narrowed consciousness, has a much bigger effect on the soul than his own plight, the soul sees clearly all the consequences of such an act, collapse and difficulties of that soul and its attempt to overcome such a negative state. The destiny of the perpetrator has more impact on the soul than the destiny of the victim. In the light of consciousness of the soul, the one who commits crime is actually the biggest loser and victim in the whole affair. Only in this world it appears as reverse.

It often takes more than one life to correct the misconception which leads to violence and evil. The perpetrator will also have to go through all the suffering and pain he caused to another person, because he between two embodiments, between two lives, receives a far higher consciousness and perception, he is faced with everything he did every moment of his life, because in the holographic universe it is inevitable. Nobody can escape himself and his deeds because everybody is what he is, everybody is individually this hologram of existence. Everything we do to others we do to ourselves. That is why we should do to others only what we want others to do to us.

Furthermore, it depends on whether this other person, the one that committed the murder, did this because of the negative states of his own consciousness, trapped in those inferior states, or he did it as a part of his program of learning and awareness. Souls go through absolutely all the possible experiences in the body, even through the violence that they commit or is committed on their body. Likewise, the experience of violence may be a part of the subject some soul needs to go through, we only acted as the assistants. It is hard to recognize the nature of such experiences, they become clearer once we exit the drama of life in the physical body.

From the reports of hypnotic regression during which people become familiarized with their past lives, there are testimonies of souls being closely knit over the lasting of several incarnations and experiencing the opposing states and experiences. Two souls in one life experience an ideal union, marriage and love, and after such a life they decide to experience the opposite states. Then one soul kills the other because of jealousy and hate, although they lived in perfect harmony the life before. Or two soulmates decide to provide one another with important experiences but through the experience of negative relationships, one was the tyrant to the other one. Therefore, the person who has the most negative influence on your life, the one that brings you big difficulties and temptations, you should see your soulmate in him/her. Soulmates more often play the hard roles to one another, than nice and gentle ones. Gentleness and pleasure (in marriage) only serve the purpose to relax us when we are on a break between two important lessons, that always requires painful tearing down the resistance of the comfort zone, tearing down the walls of the ego and mind.

There are often such cases when a soul gets used to one sex in the physical body, and it finds it hard to adjust to the body of the other sex in the next life. It is necessary for the sake of experiencing all the opposites to try out both sexes, male and female. It happens that consciousness of the soul becomes more attached to one of the sexes due to very intense experiences. When it finds itself in the body of the other sex the following time, it experiences repulsion toward the sex of the current body. They are the so-called transgender individuals, the ones that feel open rejection toward their current sex, and wish to change it. A milder symptom of the same problem, of the soul being drawn to one sex only, is when they do not hate the sex of the body they are currently incarnated in, but are attracted to the same sex. In the previous life the soul was a woman and she was attracted to men. Now it is a man, and once again, it is attracted to men. It is homosexuality. It is a question of a block that happens early on in life, while growing up and maturing. It can be successfully resolved only in hypnotic regression of past lives.

The relationship of predetermination and freedom is manifested in that the soul cannot always get the body that suits it, sometimes the body is difficult to manage, it is too conditioned by the negative astrological aspects, and the soul decides such body is a handful, and gives up on it. It seldom happens, but can happen. Such a body dies or continues to wander mechanically about. Those are the cases of severe mental patients and psychopaths. The body which has been abandoned by the consciousness of the soul to such a degree that the consciousness of the soul is unable to control it, sometimes becomes the home of conscious entities of the lower astral. Such a body is then an organic portal for various astral forces, often negative ones. All the worst crimes in this world have been committed by the organic portals, entities without a soul who use the human body. They are never committed by people with soul, because the soul sees itself, in everything, it cannot hurt itself, it is impossible, the only one who is capable of that is a being with no consciousness of the soul, who thinks that there is somebody, separate, who is unaware of the holographic unity of the overall existence. However, it is very naive to think that such organic portals can be recognized for leaving a clear fingerprint at the scene of the crime. No. There is a far bigger number of them in politics, the elites that rule this world and engage in warfare and conflicts, and they look and act like aristocrats, like cultivated people and gentry.

This would be one of the perfect explanations as to why wars exist, violence and evil, too. The issue is just about the presence or the absence of the consciousness of existence. More precisely, it is all a way of becoming aware of existence. If the divine consciousness is everything, then everything that takes place in this divine consciousness is merely awareness, perception, experience, actualization of all the possibilities of existence.

This explanation is not pleasant which does not mean it is not true. Besides, nobody said you would like all the answers to the questions of why everything is perfect.

THE DIALECTICS OF SUCCESS AND FAILURE

The following experiences which show us all the dialectics of oppositions of the perfect wholeness of existence are our personal experiences of desires and disappointments, aspirations and difficulties to realize them, will and powerlessness, freedom and slavery. Those are all the experiences every man must go through, so nicely described by Buddha in his first discourses, about suffering: uniting with what is not pleasant for us is suffering; separating from what is pleasant for us is suffering; not getting what we want is suffering; getting what we do not want is suffering. Most people have a wish for the favorable and desirable things to increase, and undesirable ones to decrease, which cannot always happen. It originates from the fact that all beings are owners of their deeds, heirs to their deeds, they arise from their deeds, are predetermined by their deeds, deeds are their sanctuary. Deeds are what divides the beings into inferior or superior, successful or unsuccessful.

All the failures we experience because we are not ideally harmonized with our higher mind and consciousness of the soul. Our higher mind sees far beyond our physical mind, it controls the events, space and time, and it does not permit desires of the lower mind to be satisfied if they are inappropriate for the development of the individual, or if they are not part of the plan of experiences in the current incarnation.

However, the principle of free will exists even for the most stupid mind in the body. It must have its free will because without it there could be no development of consciousness on the physical plane, meaning descending the consciousness of the soul in the body, the enhancement of experiences of the divine consciousness. Free will of the immature mind always tries to impose, it would like to resolve matters using 'its own will' by force, even when it thinks that it acts out of righteousness and the best intention. That is why it does not yield good results. The consciousness of the soul never imposes. It patiently awaits to be invited, recognized and accepted by the physical mind belonging to the man who lives in this world. This relationship must be mutual. Only in such a manner can the consciousness of the soul be actualized on all the levels and dimensions of existence. Only when a limited mind/ego in the physical body gets acquainted with the infinite consciousness of the divine soul, when it recognizes its small consciousness as a part of the divine consciousness, then the divine consciousness is indeed actualized everywhere, present and established like the life itself, more accurately put, life and existence are in their essence the divine consciousness itself. Once it is recognized in man who is limited to the mind, ego and body, it can never again be unaware anywhere. Then, it becomes actualized, because the man is a microcosm.

Hence, we have the dialectics of give and take, permission and prohibition interacting between the lower and the higher mind. On the one hand, the freedom to act of the individual mind limited in the body must be given, and on the other hand, not everything should be allowed, because this world would be chaos and hell, much bigger than it is already. Actually, all the negative phenomena in this world exist only due to the mind acting freely, all the negativities were committed by the mind that is insufficiently aware and is self-willed in its illusions and ignorance. All the laws and moral principles exist in this world due to the positive influence of the higher mind and consciousness of the soul, once the lower mind sees and accepts its mistakes, it repents and upgrades itself, it recognizes the impact of a higher, divine consciousness. Everything that is good in this world happens once the mind harmonizes with reality. Then the mind acts perfectly appropriately and positively because reality is always right and positive. All the best works of art and science are made then. Everything that is negative and destructive is merely a conflict of mind with reality, which means the mind is neither aware of its own nature, nor is it aware of the overall existence, at all. However, it is exactly the way in which the mind recognizes reality, by trying out its own state and ignorance. Its dialectics ranges from madness to god-knowing.

If someone has an awful-looking body, for instance, viewed from the perspective of higher consciousness of the soul which extends over all his incarnations, it is just a way for the person to disconnect from the activities it would otherwise enjoy, if he had a desirable-looking body, and focus on the sort of activities that are of intellectual or spiritual character, that are really needed in the current incarnation, which for practical reasons do not require a pretty body. It is hard to find a genius who has left an indelible trace on the destiny of humankind and who was a gorgeously-looking fellow. Difficulties with the body is the most common method used to restrain and discipline the lower mind for the benefit of cognition of the higher consciousness of the soul.

On the other hand, if someone has a great body and enjoys it to the fullest, from the higher perspective of the soul it is actually a temptation and a challenge for the person to detach from the deeper cognition, from the real work on himself/herself. Beautiful-looking people often endure bigger suffering and adversity, they cannot have real friends because other people do not see them as personalities, most people see them as objects of desire, everybody courts them and such a person often falls in the trap of temptation and uses wooing as a source of easy living, stunting their own growth in the process. Pretty women often have a much more tragic destiny than the less pretty ones, because they are the first on the list of maniacs and psychopaths, at home and in the street. Belles are often the saddest women, only nobody sees that because everybody looks at the exterior; because they have learnt to smile then when they would rather cry.

Naturally, there are handsome people who exist to make this world a more beautiful place, and more than anything else, show all the beauty human beings can have.

A similar thing applies to the material aspects of living. Money is just means to realize some intention and wish, it is energy for the manifestation of ideas. That is why immature people use money to enhance commodity and avoid discomfort, interfering negatively with their own growth. Therefore, the higher mind takes on a role of banker of the lower mind, it organizes the business expenditure because it will not leave the lower mind in charge of the finances since it would go on indulging itself. Disaster strikes every time the lower mind is in the position of power and has enough means to do as it sees fit, when it loses contact with the higher mind.

If somebody is sick it is usually a way for the lower mind to focus on cognition of the essential values of being and existence, here and now, to divert it from the mental illusions and teach it to respect life. Many have become healers upon healing themselves. That was the real reason why they were sick in the first place. It was their schooling. The lower mind usually learns the true value of something only when it loses it. It knows the most supreme truths after the lowest temptations possible. It becomes aware of freedom through restrictions. Some people come into our life to bring us something, some knowledge or experience we need. Some exit our life not to hinder our growth and acquiring the necessary experiences. People coming into our life and going out of our life are equally important and justified from the perspective of the higher consciousness. Nothing makes the man learn the truths of what surpasses the body and bodily life, and inspires him to face the reality of the soul, like somebody's untimely death, when somebody comes into your life and then quickly leaves. Therefore, we learn from everything that happens to us that there is more in life than what the eyes can see. All the imperfections of this world are just proof that there is something we do not see, some wider whole, not the imperfections of this world themselves.

Often the soul uses practical methods to weaken the attachment of the mind to the body and this world, to facilitate the human's return to their original state, as clean as possible from the impressions of life. One of the methods is old age and sickness. The feeling of powerlessness of old age and disease are good methods of slow release from existing ties to this world, a preparation for departure. This helps the dearest and nearest ones who witness the death of the loved one to prepare for the departure, as well. Death after a long illness comes like a relief. Only the sudden death of a young person is painful.

While the mind is identified with the body, its experiences are mostly bodily in nature, such people try out all the unfavorable states through physical conflicts and relationships. Their immediate surroundings directly reflect their inner state, they are untidy and negative, the social relationships are also a reflection of their unconsciousness and they are full of conflicts and rough moments, lack of mercy and understanding. Primitive and bad architecture is also a reflection of immature spirituality.

Consciousness of the soul seems to be geographically distributed in this world according to the principle of dialectics of oppositions. We are all familiar with a vast difference in mentality and spirit between the East and the West. The most supreme knowledge of soul and the divine is in the Far East. The least knowledge of the soul is in the West, on American continent. The biggest materialism rules there. Humans are just bodies – means of achieving the material goals. Anglo-Saxon Protestantism is the peak of materialism and egoism. But it has led to the consciousness of the soul through the development of material culture and social relations based on respect for human rights and liberties, the individuality. Opposed to this is the Far East, although over there the knowledge of the most subtle energies of the human being is well-preserved, the greatest science of the relationship of the lower mind and the higher consciousness of the soul, *I Ching*, and even though the human soul is there, the *atman*, turned into a religious worship, the collective consciousness and subordination toward authority is a reflection of the worst heartlessness and correspondingly big violence and emotional immaturity like in the West.

The definition of hell is that it is a place as far away from the consciousness of the soul as possible, pure materialism and the sole interest of material survival that has a view where means justify the ends. It is equally distributed all over the globe, but in various forms that reflect all the dialectics, wealth and creativity of divine perfection. Those are numerous ways that inspire the soul to express itself, and not the proof that it does not exist.

Everything always moves to achieve the union of the outer and the inner, the lower mind and the higher consciousness of the soul. All the development of life in this world exists and moves toward this harmonization.

The dialectics of success and failure has been expressed in its most perfect form in *I Ching*. All the possible situations leading to the resolution of conflict between the lower mind and the consciousness of the soul were given in this book. Humans have had only one dilemma in this world since they abandoned the cave-dwelling age: to solve the matter the way they see fit, or sit about waiting for an intervention of a higher force. The relation toward the higher force they nurtured and expressed in all possible ways ever since they can remember, through the religions and their sets of beliefs. They were all indirect ways for humans to establish the relationship with the higher consciousness, with the divine soul, with the consciousness that generates everything into existence. On the other hand, when humans relied on their intelligence to sort out existential problems, it did not always turn out well, they had to learn from all kinds of mistakes. *I Ching* is the only one that shows the ideal balance between the lower and the higher consciousness in any situation imaginable, the way we choose to act of our own accord, or when we rely on divine intervention, the influence of the higher consciousness, and how to recognize the true nature of time.

The perfection of *I Ching* is reflected in the fact that it consists of a trigram, three lines the lowest of which represents the subconsciousness, the middle one mind/ego, and the top one superconsciousness or the consciousness of the higher mind that connects us with the consciousness of our soul. There are 8 trigrams which, when joined by two in all the combinations, total 64 hexagrams. They represent the totality of all the creative processes of universe, from the genetic information to the highest phenomena and destiny of everything that takes place in life. The same way that at the base of all organic life the genetic information for its creation is present (made up from the combination of four acids: Adenine, Uracil, Guanine and Cytosine – there are sixty-four for the living world, the exact same number as the hexagrams), in the same way all the phenomena of the objective, non-organic world are not a product of chance or chaos, but the informative order of the morphogenetic fields. All the transformations that beings go through in pursuit of their destiny, and the accompanying events, are coded in the 64 hexagrams of *I Ching*. They represent the map of DNA phenomena of the world. What DNA is to organic world and the microcosm, *I Ching* is to events of the objective world, in the macrocosm. Its perfection lies in the fact that it is utilized according to the principles of the holographic universe, by random tossing of the coin or yarrow stalks casting. When we do that with the state of awareness fully concentrated on the problem, we always get the answer from the Whole. The result is no coincidence because everything is a hologram, our consciousness via the hologram, as its key player, influences the result, because consciousness is always tied with the highest, timeless outcome, ether, quantum field, where all the phenomena with all the possible outcomes are merged in unity and present in the timeless NOW. We get certain hexagrams that reveal certain situations and the way it will all play out for us. In such a way *I Ching* is just a dictionary that translates the language of the universe, the consciousness of the soul, into a language our physical mind is able to understand.[22]

In conclusion, the problem of whether to act upon our will or the will of higher consciousness, regardless of the successful or unsuccessful actions we undertake, has always been solvable in this world. People have always been given the perfect manual to use, a guide. But it has never been imposed on us, because the consciousness of the soul – the divine consciousness of the soul – does not do that. It only exists unobtrusively, all around us as well as in us. We are the ones who should recognize it.

---

[22] For a detailed explanation of *I Ching*, see my book '*I Ching: The Manual for the Correct Relationship of the Mind with the Divine Consciousness of the Soul*'

KARMIC MATURITY AND THE CIRCLING
OF DIVINE CONSCIOUSNESS

Karmic maturity of the individual consciousness through the cycle of incarnations should be understood like a holographic reflection of the manifestation of the very divine consciousness. Actually, everything is its holographic reflection, even the karmic maturity, because the universe is a hologram ruled by the anthropic principle, which means that the hologram is not impersonal; it is a precondition for the creation of the conscious subject.

We can depict the manifestation of the consciousness of the divine Absolute most accurately in the form of a sphere, the way it has always been depicted in this world, and most clearly through Platonism. Its dynamic aspect we can present like a circular route (picture 4). In this circle, it manifests itself until it reaches its ultimate distance point, the opposite point in this circle (Omega), and from that point onward it keeps returning to itself (Alpha). The manifestation away from itself is the manifestation of all the dimensions of the universe, the entire nature, and shaping the conscious subject, man, through employment of the anthropic principle, and returning to itself is the consciousness of oneself, through human self-knowledge and awakening.

It happens spontaneously, with its own inertia, once it reaches its ultimate distance point there is no other way to go than to return to itself.

The first movement of the Absolute in this manifestation, that is circling, is its current manifestation into its own opposition, the point (seed or *bindu*), the 'divine particle', and at the same time the return to itself. This first act keeps repeating and projecting itself into everything that exists in all the planes and all the dimensions, according to the principle of golden section and fractal geometry. The more it projects itself, the more those vibrations become complex and rough.

Its ultimate reach or the opposing point of manifestation of consciousness on the plane of shaping and creation is matter, its inertia and keeping the shape.

The same ultimate point in the circling of the divine consciousness in the direction of itself is manifested like a state of consciousness in the conscious subject, in man, as a state of mind which is identified with the shape, with matter and the body, and is unaware of the higher dimensions and the reality of the whole.

Throughout this entire process it is the most negative state, the most restricted state. On the outside it manifests itself in the form of inert matter. Through man it manifests like suffering, cruelty and lack of mercy. All the evil and suffering have an in common cause in the lack of consciousness. Man does not know what he does when he commits evil deeds and injustice. Any attempt to make living right and perfected is to persist in awareness, in understanding the true nature of matter and the role of consciousness in existence.

This ultimate opposition point of manifesting the divine consciousness in circling toward itself through humans is manifested as all the evil humans do as a result of their unconsciousness, like all the misunderstanding that breeds conflicts, violence and destruction. That is the so-called, rock bottom that humans experience. We tries it out always when we choose between the outer incentive and the inner conscience and consciousness; between instincts and consciousness; between blind reaction and creative action: always when we choose between good and evil, right and wrong; always when we convince ourselves that we still have time, that we can enjoy the things we are currently attracted to, and that 'next time' we will do the right thing and stick to our resolutions.

The lowest point of human existence is when a person feels enclosed into the mind and ego, and lacks awareness to extreme proportions of the fact that everything is connected in One. It later acts as the foundation of all the conflicts, with other people and the world. According to the mirror principle of the hologram, the more we are convinced that we are individuals separated from the whole, the more everything else appears to us as separate, alien, conflicted. It is not so, but we see it that way because our perception is like that; we see ourselves as being separate individuals, and therefore, we see everybody else as being separate individuals. We have an illusion that our actions are impeccable, that they are the consequences of our own will, because we are conscious even though we are unconscious, we think the same of everybody else, we think that everybody's actions are the result of their own free will, that they are aware of who they are and what they do, and that is why we condemn them. We project such a state ourselves. And this is the way in which a magic wheel of destruction, conflict and suffering is set in motion.

The closed circle of destruction will become clearer to us if we perceive it in the light of attachment of the mind/ego in the body, to the higher mind and consciousness of the soul. In the beginning of the reincarnation cycle, while the souls are still young and novel to experiences of this world, their attachment to the higher mind and the consciousness of the soul is relatively weak. The weaker this connection is, the stronger involvement of the mind/ego is, and that automatically means that the alienation of such a man from everything that is good and right is stronger. Such young souls who have not established a firm enough bond with the higher mind and consciousness of the soul yet, think that only the material life exists and there is nothing more to it, that everything is coincidence and that everything is allowed, no consequences for the acts committed there could ever be, might is right, and getting everything with the means tangible and available is the only way. It is the definition of a criminal.

Be that as it may, none of us in this world has ever been evil. It is only the mind that has drifted as far away from the consciousness of the soul as possible, without the connection to the higher mind (that is why this state is called 'eclipse of the mind'). This distance and cessation of communication between the mind in the body and the consciousness of the soul is one stage of experiences we see here as evil and destructive behavior. It is naturally the way it is, because we are not able to see then the connectedness with the other beings, we do not see the entire universe as a hologram, one divine consciousness that is life-giving to everything. Everything that is good and every understanding of what is right comes from the consciousness of the soul. Nobody becomes good, they just strengthen the bond between the consciousness of the mind in the body with higher mind and consciousness of the soul.

This state of ultimate remoteness and alienation of mind in the body from the consciousness of the soul is the only real hell, its meaning and purport. However, only from that moment onward can it turn round and come back to the road of awareness. Only from its most distant point does the circling return to its original point. This return gets expressed through humans as the awareness of their sinfulness, as repentance and the return of conscience and consciousness of the divine presence, the return to goodness and mercy.

We are controlled by the conditionality of existence and lack of awareness of existence all the way to this most distant point ever, till we reached rock bottom. Lifting from that point upward and returning to the divine consciousness is an act of free will and overcoming of conditionality.

The most important is to understand the following: only in that most distant point the complete free will exists, the full-blown freedom of existence which is so free that it allows for the oblivion of its own true nature, the awareness of itself, the oblivion of divine consciousness. Only at that point it appears that there is no divine consciousness, that all of it is just dead matter and that everything is a product of coincidence, or worse yet, a negative coincidence. Everything seems to be upside down.

This is the ultimate reach of divine creativity.

The meaning of human existence lies in our ability to recognize and keep the consciousness in this darkest, most distant corner of existence, and to regain it with our own free will and strengthen it to the point that it can come back to itself to manifest its original wholeness. If divine consciousness did everything with its own will and necessity, the entire circling of its manifestation, it would not be able to try out all the potentials of its existence, it would not experience this ultimate possibility of the complete oblivion of itself, the experience of the roughest form of conditionality and inertia which exists in the physical world and the human mind and ego which considers itself to be separate from the whole.

More than that: if the consciousness of the soul could not achieve making a come back from this most remote, unconscious state to its original conscious state *through the act of free will*, then it would achieve nothing.

The divine whole finally becomes aware of itself through us, the biggest one reflects itself in the tiniest one.[23]

For us to make this shift and find light in the worst darkness, the only thing we can do is follow the tiny thread of consciousness in ourselves, to grow in understanding of the nature of consciousness, the nature of higher dimensions, to cease accepting consciousness the way we accept everything else, like something that is on the outside, a coincidence and consequence of crude matter (the way modern science is taught in universities nowadays), but to recognize the same consciousness which is at the base of the overall existence in ourselves.

If human relationships are the issue, misunderstandings and conflicts, one should simply become aware of the consciousness in us, the one which conditions us to be aware of ourselves and with which we function, however, it is the exact same consciousness other people also have and function with. There is not a multitude of consciousnesses. The relationships will start to change and misunderstandings will be erased.

If a troubling material situation with which we are in conflict and difficulty is the issue, we should just become aware that the consciousness we have in us, which is life-giving, is the exact same consciousness that generates everything into existence, the entire nature, and all

---

[23] J. W. Goethe: 'Maxims and Reflections'

the events. This same divine consciousness is by no means passive, but it is dynamic, it creates all the events we go through, not just the natural shapes we see around us. Then the events will also start to change, our financial situation will no longer be a consequence of pure chance out of our control. When we connect the consciousness, which we are, with the consciousness which is in existence, we will be able to create events, because it is the same consciousness. This outer consciousness acted independently from our consciousness for as long as our consciousness was separate from it, suffering from the illusion of isolation from the whole, and was therefore, without the direct influence on the outer consciousness, on the events. Events and circumstances have never acted contrary to our individual consciousness because their nature is such, but only because our individual consciousness experienced it as separate and opposed. It acted like a mirror.

Actually, the nature of consciousness cannot otherwise be known since there are not various consciousnesses, but only one, the same in everything. It is the consciousness of our soul. Therefore, only with the development of spirituality man develops the consciousness. Spirituality is developed by becoming aware of the higher dimensions, because higher dimensions are a phenomenon of increasing connectedness of everything into one, into the divine whole and meaning. No matter how much man tries to develop culture and science, it is mission impossible without the consciousness of the soul, it does not lead to the divine source. That is yet another among the many freedoms man has been given: he is able to create very intelligent designs, almost identical to him, but without consciousness of the soul, hence, destructive. The reality is that the most destructive contraptions are of the most intelligent kind, but without the consciousness of the soul. It is artificial intelligence. It is destructive only if it used for what the consciousness of soul should be used, human consciousness and conscience. Without the consciousness of the soul, without the awareness of higher dimensions, any type of intelligence is nothing but the perfect aspiration to survive physically at all costs. That is the beginning of evil, closed circle within the most remote point, when consciousness gets stuck at the bottom of existence, when there is no further growing toward the divine source.

At the heart of this problem is the fact that on the most remote point away from the divine source, there is the biggest freedom of choice of the individual consciousness. The primary characteristic of the ultimate opposing point of the manifestation of the divine consciousness is the biggest freedom and independence. This feature of the most distant point is probably like this to be able to inspire the individual consciousness to make a conscious choice and return to its source, which is the absolute freedom that conditions everything. The divine absolute is complete unconditionality. A similar form of unconditionality, but to a much smaller degree, experiences the mind/ego of man. In any case, it aspires toward it in all the ways possible, but they are all wrong. For that reason, until he experiences all the wrong ways, the individual consciousness in him does not have to make a choice to return to its source, to finalize the circling, it may well remain in the illusion of its individuality, its separation from the divine, the illusion of freedom. It may go in the opposite direction. That is the essence of Satanism, or Luciferian consciousness. It is the consciousness that got itself trapped in the illusion of its own individuality, separate from the whole. Such a consciousness is the most creative in the physical world, it does not rely on unknown power and does not beg the higher force for help, it does everything that should be done by itself. However, since such a state is highly unstable, since everything else is experienced as a threat to its survival, it finds a safe haven in an ever increasing struggle for survival, in a conflict that always grows bigger, and that means a more devastating form of destruction. In such a way we have both – the maximum creativity and maximum destruction. That is yet another dialectics of perfection that is composed of the unity of oppositions.

Every act of violence and evil is looking for the wrong sanctuary and the feeling of safety. Instead of finding the right sanctuary in the divine consciousness that conditions everything, an individual consciousness searches for the feeling of safety and sanctuary in itself, in the illusion of its individuality and freedom, it puts up taller shields around itself for protection. Firstly, it puts up the physical walls when it is on the search for material safety to keep itself isolated and pleased, and secondly, it puts up psychological barriers, when it starts splitting itself and suppressing the unwanted contents into the subconscious where they have a very destructive feedback effect. It takes a little common sense to become aware of the elementary logic: if an individual exists all by itself and enjoys its own freedom of choice, how big must the will and freedom of the one who conditions everything be?

Many individual consciousness discover this logic, they find the right path to divine consciousness. They find it in the nature of the very existence, in the cognition of their own limitations and in awareness that consciousness rules over everything that exists and happens. By doing so, they surpass the illusion of their individuality: becoming aware of the fact that their own individuality and existence are actually manifestations of divine consciousness and power.

HOW TO OVERCOME OPPOSITIONS

The only way to overcome oppositions is to have the knowledge of unity which lies beyond, at the foundations of the overall existence. All the oppositions we have experienced in our lives would not be possible if there were no wider whole that conditions them. This same wider whole propels us into existence, as well. The consciousness itself which conditions our awareness of oppositions surpasses the oppositions, and this consciousness originates from the widest whole that conditions everything. It is our consciousness and our essence. Therefore, the only way for us to overcome all the oppositions is to strengthen this consciousness, our essence, the consciousness of our soul.[24]

Oppositions can be overcome in two ways only: by understanding oneself, the true nature of one's own consciousness, and understanding the nature of everything that lies beyond oneself.

Understanding oneself, that is understanding the consciousness itself.

The fact that we are aware of something is the immediate proof that we are above that what we are aware of. Consciousness is in itself the act of overcoming the object of consciousness. In identification of the consciousness with the contents of the consciousness, with the ob-

---

[24] *So that you may be the sons of your Father who is in heaven. For he makes his sun rise on the evil and on the good, and sends rain on the just and on the unjust.* (Matthew, 5.45)

jects, objective awareness is not possible. Differentiation which, at the same time, brings overcoming is needed. All our consciousness of the soul we use in the body and mind in this world we get from the consciousness of our soul. That is why only by strengthening our self-consciousness can we overcome all the oppositions. Never by fighting the opposition openly. If we fight the opposition we merely strengthen it, actually we tie ourselves to the lower dimensions where they ostensibly exist. By fighting we always descend to a bigger identification and bigger oppositions, with understanding we rise above them. The consciousness itself is a solution, it lightens up and liberates us, there is nothing else we should do with the consciousness. Self-consciousness rises above the area where oppositions happen. The consciousness itself is the goal and liberation. Because in its essence it is already above everything.

Oppositions exist only in the lower dimensions, where things and phenomena divide themselves in space and time. In the higher dimensions they more and more progressively merge in one whole (picture 1). Hence, by knowing the higher dimensions we overcome all the oppositions that rule over the lower ones only. Those higher dimensions are actually in us, they are our inner life, our unconscious. The foundation of all the other oppositions, which get manifested in life and the overall existence, is the one that exists between our conscious and unconscious being. There are no other oppositions but the one between our conscious and unconscious, between what we are aware of and what we are not aware of. It practically means that the difference between the conscious and unconscious exists only until there is ignorance of the higher dimensions of our being, the higher dimensions of existence itself. Those higher dimensions are the framework for religions and mystics, but in a way to make them unavailable to us. They are completely needlessly mystified and proclaimed out of reach and too elevated for the normal man to grasp, man is too sinful to be able to get near them, they are reserved for some higher beings and gods only. However, we are constantly in contact with the higher dimensions, we are always with them, but we are simply unaware of the phenomena, it happens to us spontaneously while we are in a dream, or are otherwise outside of our physical body. With the proper awareness of our being encompassing all the dimensions, which means with the proper practice of meditation, we remove the reason for existence of all the oppositions. Meditation is nothing but a systematic method for the awareness of all the dimensions of our being, all the dimensions of our existence, everything we are unaware of.

The understanding of the nature of everything outside of oneself.

In the absolute reality we are the holographic particle of the big unity. It practically means that we do everything to ourselves, that nothing is outside of us, but we do not see it because we are unaware of the dimensions of our being. If we were, we would see that we ourselves from our own highest dimension created all of this cosmos, this very planet we tread on unconsciously, we created all the organic conditions for sustaining life. In the end, as our final act and the most minuscule endeavor, we created our body and the intention to live in it. Actually it was all created on the part of the divine consciousness by means of our individual consciousness, first on the highest level through the archangel and angel monads of consciousness, and then through individual souls. Our soul is consciousness which is at the base of existence itself.

Existence and consciousness are one and the same thing, existence is of rough and outer nature, and consciousness is of fine and inner, but we perceive them as different due to the conditions of physical perception. We are here to forget everything because the game would not be interesting if we knew everything, we would not even participate in it if we knew everything. The truth is that we are limited in the mind and the physical body here on the ultimate opposition point of divine creation, of its circling. The ultimate opposition point is the point of the greatest oblivion of the divine, but at the same time, it is the point of its peak of creativity. The greatest creativity of the divine is the act of manifesting oneself as somebody else, as an individual who uses consciousness as its own, individual consciousness, independently of the divine source of consciousness. *We as souls came to this ultimate opposition point to push it in the right direction, upward, toward the divine source, toward the understanding of the divine consciousness, to the rounding off of the divine whole. It, on its own, would never be able to find the way home, back to itself without us. With the very presence of our souls, that come from the divine consciousness, we inspire it to recognize the right path, upward, toward the divine source.*

Once it gets lost in the ultimate opposition point of the complete freedom of unconscious activity, the manifested divine consciousness would not be able to find a way back to itself, to the divine source if there were not the presence of divine souls. It is us people who with the consciousness of our souls give meaning to this world, we remove everything that is unconscious and conscious and create. In that way we manifest the divine consciousness at work.

Actions without the inspiration of the soul in this world, on the ultimate opposition point, would be the ultimate destruction, it would be the downward slide, to an even more distant opposition point instead of the return upward, to the source. It would be an attempt to make another step forward further away from the already accomplished point of circling of the divine consciousness, which is attained in man, his mind and ego. Every further step that is not directed toward the return to the divine is pure destruction and evil, an attempt by humans to copy God. The only possible step ahead is the return to the divine source, and not for the copies to make new copies. The continuation of the circle is the movement upward, to the initial point (*bindu*) and this path leads through man, through his understanding of this entire process, the meaning of existence, through human cognition. This movement is outwardly expressed as discovering the higher dimensions, and basically it is an inner journey because all the higher dimensions are in reality human inner dimensions. In this way the discovery of the highest dimension of existence, the very divine source, is human cognition.

The first half of the circle is physical manifestation of the divine consciousness through all the dimensions, from the highest and the finest to the roughest one, down to the physical world. That would be the manifestation of cosmos, nature and the overall life. When this manifestation reaches its ultimate point, it is the appearance of man with his individual mind and ego. The continuation of the process from that most distant point is just the return to the source, ascending in the backward manner on the opposite side of that imaginary circle. ***This return does*** *not happen on the outside any more, it is now something that happens only in man, because we are dealing with the higher dimensions, and they are all within man.* The first half of the circling, the manifestation of cosmos (*prakrti*), was happening from the highest dimension toward the lowest, from the finer to the rougher. The second part is moving from the lowest to the highest, from the roughest to an increasingly finer one. The movement of the other half takes place only in man, not on the outside.

Circling of the divine consciousness from the source to the ultimate opposition point and the return to the source, can be metaphorically represented like a reflection in the mirror. The outside cosmos looks like a mirror for the divine consciousness. The inner movement is self-knowing of the observer. The outside or the manifested cosmos is in itself filled with oppositions because it is one gigantic opposition to the divine consciousness, it is its mirror. This cosmic opposition is, according to the model of the hologram, reflected in every phenomenon in the cosmos.

The only way to avoid all the oppositions of the outer cosmos is to turn toward oneself and one's own self-conscious, to strengthen the understanding and purport, and not to further get entangled in the phenomena of all the oppositions.

If we look in the mirror and see our image which is frowned and unhappy, we cannot expect the image in the mirror to stop frowning and smile before we do. We have to smile first. This image is our reflection only.

The same works for all the life situations and interpersonal relationships. If we have any expectations from the image in the mirror it simply means that we are unaware of ourselves, of our role of the conscious subject in the divine existence. We only stretch the existing oppositions more and more, instead of easing the tension by understanding the nature of events and our responsibility in them, we make the outer circumstances harder by fighting them. Since we are in the holographic universe it looks like a tug-of-war. We only waste time by evading reality, ourselves even, and making the situation harder on us. Indeed, people in this world only fight each other, it is both, the inner and the outer struggle. When one man fights with another man, he actually fights his own image in the mirror of existence. All people are mirror images to one another, because universe is a hologram and every man is only a conscious subject of such existence.

If the holographic principle is linked with the mirror metaphor it will become clear to us that reality conditions us **only to the point we let it**, only to the point we are unaware of ourselves as the subject reflecting himself in existence, existence is our image. All the illusions of man in this world and the reasons for all his suffering is the way he takes literally his mirror image, he does not know the entire process of reflecting, he considers the image to be an independent reality. We are the ones who project reality, but due to too much freedom we have on our hands, we fell into the luxury of oblivion now being unaware that we are the ones who do all of that and our comprehension of reality is that it is separate and objective and it keeps torturing and conditioning us. That is why it can condition us only to the point we allow for something like that with our own unconscious. We created our reality firstly, then forgot all about it, and now we experience our reality as something alien, outward and imposed, we adjust to it, we follow it like it is something we have to do. Even when we try to change it, it is hard for us because we do not understand the true reality, that we are the conscious subjects of everything that goes on.

If some events keep repeating it means we have not understood them properly, we have not accepted them, we have not accepted the fact that they happen just for us, for our awareness and understanding. Those are all the situations where we feel stuck, unpleasant situations, when we suffer, when the problems keep recurring. They all have one in common characteristic: we blame somebody or something on the outside, we never accept our role and responsibility, that they happen just for our sake, so that we can become aware of them and understand them. *The moment we accept circumstances and acknowledge that they happened because of us, they start to change. They do not have to go on forcing us to accept them with the proper understanding, that they are here for us*. They stop reflecting and happening, we move over to the higher realm of gathering experiences, we move on. This can be applied to all the conditions, all the life situations and interpersonal relationships. The same works for health. We can cure ourselves only if we change the paradigm, the mental grasp, because the mind rules over the whole body. There are no incurable diseases, only incurable people.

We are not responsible for what goes on beyond the horizon of our perception, on the other side of the world (unless we really caused them through some political or some other decision). Only what enters our focus is our responsibility, it happens this way so that we would become aware of it.[25] That is not always so, because there

---

[25] Information technology and the Internet make everything that goes on in the world readily available on our computer screens. That is why everything that happens globally becomes our increased re-

are so many conscious subjects, some require a certain type of experiences, and others do not, yet they are present as witnesses. Therefore, we not are responsible for absolutely everything that goes on in the world, not even our own life. We are social beings, we live together and mixing influences and experiences can happen. We invoke experiences in one another and convey influence. Everything that could possibly happen, happens.

To be able to stop the repetition of events we are stuck in, or if we maintain some monotonous situation, to be able to change it, we should first express our gratitude to them for happening to us, and by doing so we express our gratitude to the whole, acknowledging the divine consciousness for orchestrating all of that for us only, for us as the conscious subjects, so that we can become aware of the nature of this event, its significance in our system. Afterward, we should beg forgiveness from the whole for having to invest so much energy and effort to make it just for us. Certain individuals had to go through a lot and sacrifice themselves to be able to present us with

---

sponsibility, and even more so, with every passing day. That is why global events happen at an accelerated pace, and they keep being resolved just as quickly. We have run out of excuses, we can no longer pretend not to have the right information, that we need more time to find out about things. All information is available to us, and so are all the contacts. It now depends on us whether we will accept them all. This is one of the reasons why people face the consequences of their actions much quicker than before. That is why this attitude of accepting one's responsibility and the role of the conscious subject is necessary and the only possible option, for the world to be a better place to live. Now, everything is reduced to man's responsibility for understanding information and creating the correct contacts with people, on understanding one another. Indeed, what is the purpose of smart phones if our mutual communication and understanding are degrading?

the experience that is the cause of our suffering now. A lot of resources and effort were put in it, in order to create a situation that inflicts pain on us at the moment. For example, an economic crisis and war had to happen to teach you how to live properly and comfortably and become aware of the important things in life. We should ask forgiveness for all of that as an act where we show we are aware of the big sacrifice and anguish. Finally, we should express our love toward the divine whole that helped us achieve our goal to make us aware of it, so that we are able to understand and retrieve the meaning of that to the whole. We express love because we have become conscious of the fact that we have been given love in everything we were going through. That everything is perfect.[26]

In other words, we should simply become aware of existence as a kind of a mirror. It goes without saying that we must stop resisting reality firstly, it keeps happening the way it keeps happening at any given moment. If we resist it, it means we strengthen it. We strengthen everything we resist. Negative situations have no means of receiving sufficient energy for their survival except for our resistance and avoidance to accept our responsibility in the whole matter, our identification with the oppositions. It is necessary because it keeps us in the hologram. We are interconnected with everything, finely interwoven, everything individual is reflected in everything else; everything that is in everything else, is reflected in everything that is individual.

---

[26] On this healing principle see the Hawaiian teaching of Ho'oponopono. (Morrnah Simeona: *Self-Identity through Ho'oponopono, Basic 1*, Pacifica Seminars, 1990. Joe Vitale, Hew Len Ph.D.: *Zero Limits*, Wiley, 2007.) One should also consult the work of Vadim Zeland.

Therefore we should never aspire toward a new and better situation only through the negation and suppressing, as the resistance to the existing one, because the existing one is also the result of our previous actions. In this manner we simply perpetuate resistance. We cannot attract a new situation by negating the already existing one we also did our best to attract. This connection (the law of attraction) does not simply begin with our wish to make everything better, it existed before we found ourselves in this bad one. With this we created our present situation, but unconsciously. It has always existed and everything is based on it.

Apart from avoiding to resist the current situation, one needs to work on all the dimensions, and that means to overcome the material, physical realm which has a state of functioning the way it is in space and time. We must outgrow the current space and time and function from the higher plane, and in imagination (astral) we should create the desired image of reality as though it already exists, here and now. Timing is of crucial importance, we should envisage clearly that it is not some future event we aim to materialize, but the reality that is here and now – although only in make believe world for now.

On the physical plane it looks as though it is some fancy and a waste of time, but it is in reality work on the higher dimensions that have a very creative effect on our dimension, our physical reality. It is no fantasy, but creative action. This imagination (astral) should be teamed with will, energy, fervor and passion (fire) in order to create the desired image, to enjoy it with passion we would have if it really existed in the physical realm. Above all, one should be consistent in his thoughts, ideas (air) so that the idea we wish to make true is perfectly clear down to the last detail, that we never begin to doubt it is the reality we create in higher dimensions, and that it will materialize onto this plane, this physical realm, our reality.

The greatest challenge on the physical plane is the ability to accept change, not the way we imagined them, but the way they come on their own. If we wish to receive something from the higher dimensions, from the higher consciousness, then we should accept the simple logic that our higher consciousness knows how to do something better than we do. We found ourselves in the problem because we are not skilled enough to resolve it. Therefore, we should not advise the higher consciousness on how to do stuff and imply ways in which to come up with the solution, we should do better to simply stick to the idea and visualize our final goal. We should leave the details to the divine whole that knows everything best, not only how to do things, but whether we need them in the first place. If we fall short of our expectations with all the books of the law of attraction we have read so far, it means it is not something our soul requires as the plan for the current life, or we have not begun to function on all the dimensions yet.

Everything that is created on the higher dimensions is implemented on the lower ones. That is the law of creation. We are successful in implementing it when we learn to use it on all the dimensions, in its entirety. The existing bad reality we have now we have created, albeit unconditionally. The only reason we do not see effects of this law is because we do not use it whole, it will not come true if we only fantasize about the desired goal and do very little or nothing to make it happen, if we want (fire) one thing, think (air) about something else, fantasize (water) about something completely different, and do (earth) nothing in connection with the previous three. In the physical reality nothing will materialize. On the physical plane the only thing that comes true is what has in a synchronized way encompassed all the dimensions, from an idea to the realization. [27]

Together with the skill of accepting change there is the problem of time. There is always temptation of time when nothing seems to be happening, when we have doubts as to whether the thing works, at all. We create this time gap because we have not applied ourselves to the goal properly in all the dimensions. We do not see our own subconscious, we do not see that it still does not operate in a unanimous manner. Time is the gap between an idea and its realization. In reality, in the wholeness of existence, there is no time, everything is just present moment. In order to accomplish things we need to remove time, and that means to unite all the dimensions of action, here and now, every moment of every day. Instead of experiencing dark moments because nothing seems to be happening, we would do ourselves a favor by spending time raising the level of our awareness and learning to perfect functioning on all the dimensions, at any given moment.

Apart from functioning on the higher dimensions one should function on the physical realm, in accordance with the physical laws. With the help of the physical laws we become able to accept changes that lead us toward accomplishing our goal, our preferred reality. Since we exist in the holographic universe, we must be the change we

---

[27] Functioning in all the dimensions of existence and our being, from mind to energy and feelings to the body itself, was described in the Bible as the first commandment of God: " *And thou shalt love the Lord thy God with all thy heart, and with all thy soul, and with all thy mind, and with all thy strength.*" (Marc 12. 30)

expect from the outside to happen to us. This is the way how to exert influence in the physical dimension. We must do things to others we wish to happen to us. That is the only way for us to see what we want to see in the mirror of existence. If we wanted to have a bigger and a better house, we should help other people get a house; if we want money, we should give it to those who need it. If we want to be loved, we should give love. We should give first, and always a lot. This is a way for us to prove that we are aware of the whole and the higher force as our guide, the consciousness of the soul and divine consciousness. This is a way in which we enable the divine consciousness to act through us, consciousness of the soul always acts out of plenty and without doubts because it has divine whole behind, it knows there are no losses anywhere.[28]

This is a way for us to act in perfect harmony with the consciousness of our soul, because we always gain with it.

The oppositions can be overcome by understanding oneself and the nature of reality that lies beyond ourselves.

---

[28] Matthew, 5. 38-48.

THE PERFECTION OF SPIRITUAL PRACTICE

We cannot avoid being in a spiritual practice in this world because everything is consciousness in the holographic universe. We are conscious subjects of the objective existence and everything happens for us to make sense of phenomena. There is a big illusion that spiritual practice is reserved only for mystics and monks, so-called religious people. They are as far away from the spiritual practice as possible. The true spiritual practice happens always and everywhere because nothing can be outside the divine Absolute.

The oldest spiritual practice is tantra. Tantra is a part of the most ancient spiritual practice which is known as the "fourth way" brought to the west by G.I. Gurdjieff, and elaborated by his disciple P.D. Ouspensky.[29] It is a practice of becoming fully aware of everything that IS at any given moment, no choice available, it entertains the attitude that everything is divine consciousness already and it only needs to be made aware of, more accurately, its presence must be actualized. Nothing else. Tantra works with all kinds of consciousness in man, that are manifested as psychoenergetic centers in human beings in the form of chakras. It starts from the most rudimentary level, and that is control of energy through the exchange between sexes, sexuality, and uplifts itself to all the other energy exchange forms, social interaction, rela-

---

[29] P. D. Ouspensky: The fourth way

tionship toward the world, nature, thought, self-knowing.

Tantra is the aspiration to preserve the consciousness of the soul in all the forms of phenomena found in man, from the lowest, elementary and instinctive ones, to the highest mental states. Tantra is an aspiration of the consciousness of the soul to resist all the challenges and temptations that might arise while it is in the body, to preserve the consciousness of itself, not to fall for the identification with events. Therefore, not to escape challenges, but directly experience them all the way through, the way they are, and overcome them as such: with understanding and experience. It is the aim and the purpose of every human life, of all the human dramas and all the karma, all the human work in this world. Tantra is a way of speeding up this process and its better understanding.

Planet Earth is training ground for the souls in *agora tantra*. *Agora tantra* is the final extreme kind of tantra that tests all the ultimate states of body and mind, death even. In all the extreme states they have their purpose to keep the transcendental consciousness of the soul, to be aware of themselves always. Once they achieve this they then surpass being born and dying, the reasons for reincarnation, the consciousness of the soul recognized itself in all the possible shapes, in existence itself. The principle is in the following: if we manage to preserve the consciousness of the soul in the most extreme cases the body and mind can find themselves in, then we become the masters of the body and mind, then the body and mind cannot trap us in their limitations even in those states which are less extreme. Thus, the need for incarnations stops.

Everything people do in this world is a mild form of tantra. Every farmer in the field, worker in a factory or a coal mine, a mechanic smeared with oil, a technician at the office who cannot stand his boss and colleague – is a spiritual practitioner of tantra, an elite school of consciousness, only nobody bothered to inform them about it. Successful and happy people, same as unhappy and unsuccessful, are practitioners of the same tantra, only in varying stages of experience. The dialectics of oppositions manifests itself in space and time, in certain places and moments, not all at once and not the same everywhere.

Opposition is reflected in the so-called spirituality. Since it is all only divine consciousness trying itself out in all the ways possible, there is nothing which is not it itself, therefore, there is nothing that is not spiritual, or divine. The appearance of religious and spiritual practices consequently have dual, often opposite meaning and sense. The former serves to remind the unconscious man who he is and what the nature of existence is, that it is divine. The latter is that, if the divine itself exists, such aspirations are necessarily contradictory in themselves and have a counterproductive effect, they distance the man away from the consciousness of himself and the divine itself.

Man builds temples, prays and worships deity, and at home he is a tyrant. However, existence itself is as divine as could be, every particle is divine. The first religious communities were merely a gathering of spiritually like-minded individuals, for example, the early Christian Gnostic communities *ecclesia*, which were spontaneous gatherings of people and who were against closing off divine presence into certain buildings (Acts of the Apostles 7.48-49; 17.24), because they were against any idolatry. When people lost the direct relationship toward divine, the church theocratic institution came into being, and placed God solely within the confinements of their church and their estate.

Instead of focusing all our attention, respect and consciousness on the religious objects and symbols we should focus them on every thing we see and touch, on all the people and all the beings, because all of them are the reflection of divine consciousness, the divine presence. Man became more cultivated and better through the very respect and admiration he expressed toward the divine nature of the life itself. Religions only prevent him from doing that. If he has become better because of the religion and faith, he became so only because he recognized the religious teaching and applied it on his own life, connecting himself to the Whole. If people directed 10% of their consciousness they invest into religious rituals in temples into their dear ones and the world around them, this world would be heaven. No, that is the wrong estimate. Mere 1% would do.

There is no way for the man to be truly religious without seeing and respecting the divine in everything, in his home firstly, in communication with the close members of his family, to try to make his home his castle, the holy relics should be all the objects and tools he holds in his hand, his prayer should not be a dirge but an expression of gratitude for all, he should express his gratitude to God by means of working and he should always be aware that it is not him who works, but God works through him, his altar should be every good thing he has made, the only sacrifices he makes should be those of his pride and ignorance, the only communication with God should be the forgiving understanding of thy neighbor, the only devotion to God should be devotion to every living being. Until it becomes this way, all the temples and religions will exist as the cover for all the hypocrisy and self-deception, justification for all the conflicts. Indeed, if the divine consciousness is at the base of all existence, why single it out, respect and worship it only in special edifices, why distinguish it from every living being, why distinguish it from ourselves even? The answer is simple: because we are not aware of our true nature and the nature of the divine, and everything that is unconscious is projected outwardly, into some objects.

Because man is unconscious this world is ruled by paradoxes. Nothing distances man in this world from the consciousness of the divine presence more than religions do, although they are the ones that pull him close to God the most. Nothing in this world is more violent than religions and more aimed at non-violence, more filled with stupidity and lies, and at the same time more true than religions. The most religious people on this planet are Taliban who give their life for their faith, they kill their own children even if they do not serve their faith. However, nuclear physicists are closer to the divine consciousness, they are atheists, they make atomic bombs and they themselves would never murder anyone, they advocate the rule of law and world peace, in their work and knowledge they are the closest to the original, divine principles of nature, and yet they know nothing about the soul.

This crazy dance has been going on for too long in this world.

A monk renouncing life and creating for himself the ideal conditions in order to know the divine, distances away from God the most, because divine is in everything and everything is divine. A monk indulges himself by avoiding the oppositions, by imitating and rituals. Unlike him, the divine is recognized much quicker and more directly by a common housewife taking care of her family, or a single mother who works all day long to be able to feed her children, she sees divine directly in her child and only that gives her enough strength to fight as bravely as a lion with all the difficulty that she has even in her own home very often, with her next of kin.

It is all the practice of the "fourth way" or tantra, but unfortunately of the unconscious kind. All it takes for the true 'spiritual practice' is to make the unconscious conscious. Nothing else. Practice always takes place of its own accord.

Practice is general and sometimes the reverse can happen. There are monks that know the presence of divine consciousness directly, the same way that there are bad housewives. The reason for both is the same: dialectics of oppositions. A monk believes himself to be alienated from the divine and in need of merging, he suffers because he does not see that it has been in him all that time. Mother receives all her strength from the child, and fails to see that it is nothing but a tiny window of consciousness of the divine trying to get through to her, it is the real source which gives her strength and joy despite all the misfortune. Divine should not be limited to anything because it is in everything. Everything we find attractive and endearing is such only due to the consciousness of the soul that manifests itself through it, and not the external shape it becomes manifested through. The external shape can be quite phenomenal. Gems of soulfulness may be found in the worst human gutter.

That is the reason it is said that we are sinners in this world, by sinning we actually become aware of what is right, we become alert to the correct and perfect approach to life. Christ came to show us our position with his testimony of the pure consciousness of the soul. That is why compassion toward the biggest sinner is the closest a person can get to the divine consciousness. Nobody has become a saint without experiencing the sin first. The same goes for the society on the whole, for the situation in the world. It is wrong on so many levels, but only because of the fact that it is the only way to reach awareness of the proper way of life, injustice exists only for the true polity and justice to be established, chaos exists so that things could be put in order.

When disaster strikes, when we let go of our 'spiritual practice', mediation, if we had one, at all, and start to wander aimlessly, that, too, is part of the practice. Practice never stops because divine consciousness always exists in everything. During the meditation we experience presence in reality, but only in its silent and abstract form. When after the meditation difficulty of work and uncertainty of life befall us, we experience this reality in a concrete way. There are not multitudes of realities, it is one and the same in everything, in the deepest ecstasy of *samadhi*, in god-knowing, in *nirvana*, in the worst living conditions and temptations. All the enlightened ones (*bodhisattva*) tell us that we are already in *nirvana*.[30]

Then when we are lost, rejected from the comfort zone and our habits, we experience our contact with the higher consciousness of the soul, its functioning from the outside, which we with our own mind tend to experience as higher force or the unknown, and as uncertainty. Are we ready to accept the divine as unknown, unexpected, and even the least desirable? If divine is at the base of everything, it can reach out to us from literally everything. It always does, it is always here. It is closer to us than anything else in the world, then when we think it is the most distant. It seems that the divine entertains itself by testing us through a myriad of situations and unexpected

---

[30] *Diamond sūtra* (Sanskrit: *Vajracchedikā Prajñāpāramitā Sūtra*)

shapes so that we learn to recognize and accept it. Until the point we accept it in absolutely everything.

There is not one direct path to the divine. The road is always right, both when it is direct and indirect because nothing is outside the divine, all roads lead to it, all roads are emanation of the divine.[31] Everything is already divine. That is why one should only be perfectly aware of every road, of every event, of every moment in everything, regardless of the shape and state of affairs, one should always enjoy this present moment to the fullest. Taking part in the journey with our whole being maximally consciously is all that it takes. Only then the road disappears and we have reached the finish line. If we travel toward the divine projecting it through space and time the same way we do with the rest of the mundane issues, we will never be able to reach our goal, its end. If the purpose of the spiritual journey we do not realize here and now, we will never be able to realize it.

This is the ultimate paradox and opposition in the dialectics of spirituality: we realize divine presence through the awareness of losing it, through mistakes and wandering, because all the time we are in it, and we can never be outside it. This is why we can wander, why we have the freedom to do wrong. We ourselves are the divine consciousness that knows itself in all the possibles shapes. What appears to us here as wrong and evil, suffering and wandering through the valley ignorance, poverty and loss, from the aspect of divine consciousness is noth-

---

[31] "I Am the Way, the Truth, and the Life" said Jesus, but the emphasis here is at the very beginning of his answer "I Am", focusing on the consciousness of one's essence, the Self, the consciousness of the soul. The road disappears because it was in us, and we have reached our goal. It is always here and now, never in the future or somewhere else.

ing but manifestation of its most extreme possibilities in all the details. It is all its manifested creativity. The moment we become aware of it and accept all the adversity and temptations as godsent, the situation changes. When we act in harmony with the divine consciousness (*tao*) we act creatively then, we create reality, we are no longer its objects, but its conscious subjects. Divine consciousness realizes itself through all of these, through all of the available shapes and states.

Divine consciousness is superior to all the phenomena. Our consciousness is offshoot of the same divine consciousness. When through our consciousness we accept divine consciousness and take part in it, we then take part in this power of creating phenomena.

There is no imperfection or the loss of anything. Only man who does not have awareness of the divine presence and perfection feels helpless and thinks he is at a loss.

Such true spirituality we learn from life. It is the teaching of the "fourth way", the practice of the Sufis,[32] Gurdjieff and Don Juan (in the works of Castaneda) arranged such circumstances to their disciples, they made them be aware of every moment and accept all the challenges with no possibility of choosing or avoiding, most often the ones they do not want and, therefore avoid. This awareness with no choice offered and no avoidance that must be practiced at every given moment and state of ex-

---

[32] However, it is not the practice of Islam. Sufism should by no means be equated with Islam. Sufism is much older than Islam. Islam was created with the goal of destroying Sufism, Muslims killed Sufi mystics, but the spirituality of Sufism is so authentic and strong that it has lived on by being partially assimilated into Islam, although in a distorted and ruined form.

istence is the base of the Buddhist meditation, *vipassana* and *satipatthana*.

The perfection of spiritual practice is based on existence itself because our entire being is designed for such practice. Existence and consciousness are one and the same thing, but they get manifested separately through the four dimensions and seven phases. Our physical body, emotions, will and the mind are comprised of the dimensions of existence. Our body unites the energy of existence with the consciousness through the seven phases, and they are manifested through seven psychoenergetic centers or chakras. Our being is a microcosm, which means it contains everything required for the perfect union of consciousness and existence, it is perfectly designed for the merging of every individual consciousness (mind) with the absolute consciousness of the divine. Through the seven phases and four dimensions the consciousness of the divine disperses itself into all the individual phenomena. It through the body splits into the world of illusion and through the same body it unites into the original whole. The same mechanism, the human body, divides the consciousness into the illusion of multitude only to merge it with the original unity again. It is the same process which manifests in two ways, the absolute and the relative one.

The human body is so perfectly designed that it is able to conduct automatically the consciousness of the absolute away from all the individual experiences all the way to the return to its original unity. This conducting is best manifested as the movement of consciousness and energy from the first upward to the highest chakra. However, the quality of free will, manifested in the most distant opposition point of manifestation (more on that in the final chapter, picture 4), creates the possibility of keeping the consciousness more in the experience of existence reflected by the first three lowest chakras. Therefore, if man did not waste time and energy on being focused on the first three chakras, consciousness would automatically, of its own accord, rise all the way to the top chakra, to the return to the divine absolute. Such experiencing the consciousness in the roughest phases of experiences, the first three chakras, can last for several lifetimes, it constitutes all the karmic experiences. Body is designed in a way that it automatically conducts the divine consciousness through our entire body, through all the chakras. Man experiences his individual will and consciousness to extreme limits by experiencing the freedom provided by the first three chakras. Once he has had enough of that, he decides to allow the consciousness to rise to the highest chakra. This is all that is required to know about spiritual practice.

SHIVA'S ADVICE FOR RECOGNIZING PERFECTION

The practice by which we align with reality and know the perfection of every moment, can be reduced to attaining the timeless present. It is a practice of calming down the mind from any kind of contents, all the thoughts, that pull us into some imaginary time, that further pull us away from reality, which exists only in present moment. Calming the mind down from all the contents or thoughts is the practice of meditation, whereas meditation is only the finishing and final practice, the true practice is life every moment of every day. Everything that happens to us every moment of our life is meditative practice, the practice of awareness of existence and coming to know the functioning of the mind. Thus, life is the practice of experiencing all the identifications with the mind for the sake of becoming acquainted with the consciousness that lies beyond the mind, which is precondition for the mind and thus life.

The calming of the mind entails attaining the most supreme and the most subtle dimension of existence, *akasha* or ether, the universal quantum field. This highest and finest dimension everything else is manifested from, always exists in us, it gives us all the awareness we possess. To open ourselves up for its presence, to be able to use the original consciousness actively, all we should do is stop interfering with the activities of the lower dimensions, thoughts (air), energy fluctuation (fire), imagination and desires (water), and identification with the human body. Then, when it stops being interfered with by the lower and rougher activities, it bursts out through our consciousness as the awareness of the self, our essence, it displays itself as the true nature of existence itself, it reveals itself in everything. Everything we see is only the manifestation of the divine consciousness that conditions everything. All that we do, all the activities we perform in our physical life are merely rehearsals to be able to express the divine consciousness of our soul into existence in a creative way, to learn to preserve it in the face of all temptation of the lower and rougher shapes of existence. The lower and rougher the shape of existence is, the more the consciousness is caught in certain forms of conditioning and they, therefore, slow down the consciousness. On the roughest plane, the physical world, consciousness is so conditioned that it functions like in a dream.

All the dimensions of existence can best be understood as different speeds of manifestation of one and the same divine consciousness. In the dimension of air or thoughts it is very fast, it can alter its shapes and contents instantly; in the dimension of fire or energy and will, it is slower, attached to a certain shape or motivation, contents; in the dimension of water it is even slower due to its attachment to the shape although it is still easily changeable, but slower than in the higher dimensions; in the element of earth or the physical dimension, it is at its slowest. The slowest divine consciousness is everything we see around us as the rough physical shape or matter. Every physical object is only maximally slowed down divine consciousness or the vibration of the 'divine particle'.

Man can awaken only if he recognizes that the physical world does not exists all by itself and for itself but it is only a reflection of the divine consciousness, its possibility to manifest itself in such a way, as rough physical reality. Being awaken is being conscious. Therefore, recognizing that everything is consciousness gives alertness. It is easy to recognize higher dimensions as consciousness, the point of living is to recognize the roughest forms of existence as consciousness, that all the dimensions and forms of existence we get to recognize as divine consciousness, and as our consciousness, as well. We are able to achieve this by perfecting our own consciousness, that is wakefulness.

This practice is the oldest in the world. Its goes so far back in history that its origin is unknown. This practice has reached us as the science of tantra. It exists in various shapes globally, scattered across many traditions. All true spiritual practices have their background in *tantrism*, but have been modified to a bigger or a lesser degree to suit people of varying states of consciousness and karmic maturity.

The oldest symbol which depicts the divine consciousness is the figure of a man sitting in lotus position, as a yogi, he has three faces, there are motifs of animals and nature around him. It was the figure from the Indus-Valley, Mohenjo Daro. It is about ten thousand years old. However, it was merely a southern part of the much older Slav-Aryan civilization that spanned the entire Asia, Western Europe and Sumer. The dead were buried in the same position in Lepenski Vir, Vinca, in Serbia.

The image of deity with three faces always represents the highest principle of existence, *akasha* or ether, the quantum consciousness. The three faces are past, present and future, that is the timeless present that encompasses the remaining three. Often this depiction is with three or more arms, which denotes a versatile activity, the primordial divine consciousness manifesting and functioning in a myriad of ways, it has an effect with innumerable arms on everything that goes on, the divine consciousness is in charge of everything.

The purest depiction of such a deity is Shiva. He has three faces, multiple arms, and is represented as a dancer. The very purpose of presenting Shiva as a dancer (*Shiva Nataraj*) is to show us that divine consciousness is one with existence, that existence and divine are one and the same only in their different states, consciousness as the unmanifested and existence as manifested state of the identical nature. The same way the dancer always exists, both when he dances and when he is motionless, the same divine consciousness manifests itself as everything that exists, or is peaceful inside. It is always the same, it itself, whether it is in its manifested or the unmanifested state, dancing or being still. Divine is manifested as cosmos, as the dance, and its essence is ever-present in everything, the same way the dancer is present in the dance, and there can be no dance without the dancer. It is depiction of the 'divine particle' and its dance through the instantaneous vibrations of everything that exists. In everything that happens only it happens alone.

It is said that Shiva intermittently creates and destroys, produces the world and reabsorbs it in the perpetual happening, the iconography is represented with a dance move: Shiva is holding a drum in his hand, the symbol of creation through vibration, and the flame in his other hand, the fire that destroys universe at the end of time, but also illuminates it with the light of consciousness. Therefore, the drum is vibration of one 'divine particle', and fire is its energy that conducts the light of consciousness. The oldest original Slav-Aryan depiction of Shiva was that it all happens instantly in the timeless present, it is the 'divine particle'. Over time on the Indian subcontinent this correct depiction was lost and dimmed by the illusion of huge time cycles. It was all put in the context of linear time to satisfy the imagination of believers and hide the true nature of reality, of the timeless present of divine consciousness which is everything, which means that it is us alone, here and now. Nothing else exists not could there ever be. We are it. However, this oblivion makes sense in the fact that it is necessary for the human life drama to take place, and for individual souls in this world, but only in the illusion of linear time. It is all intent and plan by the divine consciousness to experience itself in its most distant state, in the complete oblivion of itself, in the human mind and ego, in this physical world.

***

The following text *Centreing* is taken from the Paul Rep's book: *Zen Flesh, Zen Bones*, Pelican books 1972. (Paul Reps, Zen Flesh, Zen Bones, A Collection of Zen and Pre-Zen Writings). This book is a collection of Zen writings, and the last text, "Centreing" – which belongs to tantric tradition according to Rep's claim – found its way here, because in his opinion, it contains some of the ideas so typical for Zen. The writing is also known as *Vijñāna Bhairava Tantra*.

"Wandering in the ineffable beauty of Kashmir, above Srinagar, I come upon the hermitage of Lakshmanjoo, who shared with me the teachings, presented in this text", says Reps. According to Lakshmanjoo's claims, the writings are derivative of the teachings from *Vigyan Bhairava Tantra*, *Sochanda Tantra* and *Malini Vijaya Tantra*. Both him and Reps translated them from Sanskrit into English. Reps claims that *tantras* this text is compiled from, were written 4.000 years ago.

The divine couple, whose dialogue begins this text, symbolizes two basic forms of energy. Shakti (goddess, Devi) signifies the kinetic functional energy aspect, which creates the changeable picture book, whereas, Shiva signifies the potential, universal aspect of energy beyond any function or manifestation, pure being out of time. Shakti is energy which conditions and maintains everything, and Shiva is divine consciousness that is at the base of energy. Shiva is finer and Shakti is a rougher state of one and the same thing. Shiva is inner and Shakti is the outer manifestation of one and the same thing. Shiva is absolute and Shakti is relative. Those two represent pure existence in all its forms and dimensions.

These 112 *sutras* are divided in three groups. The first group refers to chakra awakening, the second one to using *mantras*, and the third one to meditation. There are also *sutras* which through an esthetic experience reveal the very existence as divine consciousness.

Meditation in a narrower sense (*dhyana*) makes up for the greater part of the text. Those are *sutras* that refer to: 1) uniting with the world, 2) esthetic perception, 3) developing consciousness, 4) cessation of the stream of consciousness and 5) surpassing (transcendence).

Surpassing is becoming aware of the true nature of the manifested energy forms. This can be achieved with the growing awareness, when allure and attachment to the emergent world wanes.

The unity of consciousness and existence happens throughout all the cosmos and all the emergent life forms. The final union of comprehending the meaning of everything happens only in man. It happens in seven phases, which are manifested through the seven chakras or states of consciousness, seven modalities of uniting consciousness and existence. The science of tantra is actually becoming aware and experiencing personally the unity of consciousness and existence, in all the states of consciousness, in all the modalities of existence.

There is a false teaching about tantra which says that the goal is to awaken the primordial energy, *kundalini*, and make it rise to the top chakra. In the perfect reality the truth is different from the one we are served in the media. There is no rising of energy because it is everywhere. Consciousness is the most subtle existence and existence is the roughest state of one and the same thing, and energy is in between them, as their middle phase. Energy binds consciousness and existence. It is the manifestation of both aspects, and it means that it is already present in everything as consciousness and existence. The issue is only to understand it consciously and by doing so harmonize it throughout all the phases of manifestation.

Tantra teaches us that in every chakra the unity of consciousness and existence takes place, not only in the lowest one when we experience orgasm. In the second chakra this unity is expressed through sexual union with another being; in the third one it is realization of joint goals in life irrelevantly of personal interests; union of consciousness and existence in the fourth chakra is manifested as the orgasm of pure love with existence, the unity of consciousness and existence is experienced emotionally, independently of the body. In the fifth chakra consciousness of existence can be verbalized mentally, not only experienced emotionally, the orgasm of wise words and cognition happens here; in the sixth chakra the orgasm of intuitive insight takes place which surpasses all the words and reflection pieces. In the seventh chakra we finish with all the illusions of the separation between consciousness and existence.

In the following text Shiva advises us how to recognize the perfect union of consciousness and existence in all the possible ways through all the chakras: esthetically, in the beauty of existence alone, through the fourth chakra more accurately; in between two thoughts or through the sixth chakra; in between two breaths or through the third chakra. It is hard to distinguish between all the methods and identify them with all the chakras because many of them are entwined and interconnected. The aim is to join all the chakras in one consciousness of the eternally present perfection of existence, for the perfection of existence to manifest through man on all the levels of consciousness, that is chakras. When consciousness and existence are connected in all the chakras evenly, it is called *samadhi*, which means merging or centering.

CENTERING
Vijñāna Bhairava Tantra

Devi asks:

O Shiva, what is your reality?
What is this wonder-filled universe?
What constitutes seed?
Who centers the universal wheel?
What is this life beyond form pervading forms?
How may we enter it fully, above space and time, names and descriptions?
Let my doubts be cleared!

Shiva replies:

1. Radiant One, this experience may dawn between two breaths. After breath comes in and just before turning up – the beneficence.

2. As breath turns from down to up, and again as breath curves up to down - through both these turns, realize.

3. Or, whenever in-breath and out-breath fuse, at this instant touch the energy-less, energy-filled center.

4. Or, when breath is all out and stopped of itself, or all in and stopped - in such universal pause, one's small self vanishes. This is difficult only for the impure.

5. Attention between Eyebrows, let mind be before thought. Let form fill with breath essence to the top of the head and there shower as light.

6. When in worldly activities, keep attention between two breaths, and so practicing, in a few days be born anew.

7. With intangible breath in center of forehead, as this reaches the heart at the moment of sleep, have direction over dreams and over death itself.

8. With utmost devotion, center on the two junctions of breath and know the knower.

9. Lie down as dead. Enraged in wrath, stay so. Or stare without moving an eyelash. Or suck something and become the sucking.

10. While being caressed, Sweet Princess, enter the caress as everlasting life.

11. Stop the doors of the senses when feeling the creeping of an ant. Then.

12. When on a bed or a seat, let yourself become weightless, beyond mind.

13. Or, imagine the five coloured circles of the peacock tail to be your five senses in illimitable space. Now let their beauty melt within. Similarly, at any point in space or on the wall - until the point dissolves. Then your wish for another comes true.

14. Place your whole attention in the nerve, delicate as the lotus thread, in the center of your spinal column. In such be transformed.

15. Closing the seven openings of the head with your hands, a space between your eyes becomes all-inclusive.

16. Blessed One, as senses are absorbed in the Heart, reach the center of the lotus.

17. Unminding mind, keep in the middle – until...

18. Look lovingly at some object. Do not go to another object. Here in the middle of the object - the blessing.

19. Without support for feet or hands, sit only on the buttocks. Suddenly the centering.

20. In a moving vehicle, by rhythmically swaying, experience. Or in a still vehicle, by letting yourself swing in slowing invisible circles.

21. Pierce some part of you nectar filled form with a pin, and gently enter the piercing and attain to the inner purity.

22. Let attention be at a place where you are seeing some past happening, and even your form, having lost its present characteristics, is transformed.

23. Feel an object before you. Feel the absence of all other objects but this one. Then leaving aside the object-feeling and the absence-feeling, Realize

24. When a mood against someone or for someone arises. Do not place it on the person in question, but remain centered.

25. Just as you have the impulse to do something, Stop.

26. When some desire comes, consider it. Then, suddenly, quit it.

27. Roam about until exhausted and then, dropping to the ground, in this dropping be whole.

28. Suppose you are gradually being deprived of strength or of knowledge. At the instant of deprivation, transcend.

29. Devotion frees.

30. Eyes closed, See your inner being in detail. Thus see your true nature.

31. Look upon a bowl without seeing the sides or the material. In a few moments become aware.

32. See as if for the first time a beauteous person or an ordinary object.

33. Simply by looking into the blue sky beyond the clouds, the serenity.

34. Listen while the ultimate mystical teaching is imparted. Eyes still, without blinking, at once, become absolutely free.

35. At the edge of a deep well look steadily into its depths until the wondrousness.

36. Look upon some object, Then slowly withdraw your sight from it, Then slowly withdraw your thought from it.

37. Devi, Imagine Sanskrit letters in these Honey filled foci of awareness, First as letters, Then more subtly as sounds, Then as most subtle feeling. Then, leaving them aside, be free.

38. Bathe in the center of sound, As in the continuous sound of a waterfall. Or, by putting the fingers in the ears, Hear the sound of sounds.

39. Intone a sound, As AUM . Slowly, As sound enters soundfulness, So do you.

40. In the beginning and gradual refinement of the sound of any letter, Awake.

41. While listening to stringed instruments, Hear their composite central sound; Thus omnipresence.

42. Intone a sound audibly, Then less and less audibly As feeling deepens Into this silent harmony.

43. With mouth slightly open, Keep mind in the middle of the tongue. Or, as breath comes silently in, Feel the sound HH.

44. Center on the sound AUM Without any A or M.

45. Silently intone a word ending in AH. Then in the HH, Effortlessly, the spontaneity.

46. Stopping ears by pressing And the rectum by contracting, Enter the sound.

47. Enter the sound of your name And, through this sound, All sounds.

48. At the start of sexual union Keep attentive on the fire in the beginning, And so continuing, Avoid the embers in the end.

49. When in such embrace your senses are shaken as leaves, Enter this shaking.

50. Even remembering union, Without the embrace, Transformation.

51. On joyously seeing a long-absent friend, Permeate this joy.

52. When eating or drinking, Become the taste of food or drink, And be filled.

53. O lotus eyed one, Sweet of touch, When singing, seeing, tasting, Be aware you are and discover the Everliving.

54. Wherever satisfaction is found, In whatever act, Actualize this.

55. At the point of sleep, When the sleep has not yet come And the external wakefulness vanishes, At this point Being is revealed.

56. Illusions deceive, Colors circumscribe, Even divisibles are indivisible.

57. In moods of extreme desire Be undisturbed.

58. This so-called universe Appears as a juggling, A picture show. To be happy, look upon it so.

59. O Beloved, Put attention neither on pleasure nor on pain, But between these.

60. Objects and desires Exist in me as in others. So accepting, Let them be transformed.

61. As waves come with water And flames with fire, So the Universal waves with us.

62. Wherever your mind is wandering, Internally or externally, At this very place, this.

63. When vividly aware Through some particular sense, Keep in the awareness.

64. At the start of sneezing, during fright, In anxiety, above a chasm, flying in battle, In extreme curiosity, at the beginning of hunger, At the end of hunger, Be uninterruptedly aware.

65. The purity of other teachings Is an impurity to us. In reality, Know nothing as pure or impure.

66. Be the unsame same to friend as to stranger, in honor and dishonor.

67.   Here is the sphere of change, change, change. Through change consume change.

68.   As a hen mothers her chicks, mother particular knowings, particular doings, in reality.

69.   Since, in truth, Bondage and freedom are relative, These words are only for those Terrified with the universe. This universe is a reflection of minds. As you see many suns in water from one sun, So see bondage and liberation.

70.   Consider your essence as light rays From center to center up the vertebrae, And so rises livingness in you.

71.   Or in the spaces between, Feel this as lightning.

72.   Feel the cosmos as a translucent ever-living presence.

73.   In summer when you see the entire sky Endlessly clear, Enter such clarity.

74.   Shakti, See all space as if already Absorbed in your own head In the brilliance.

75.   Waking, sleeping, dreaming, Know you as light.

76.   In rain during a black night, Enter that blackness As the form of forms.

77.   When a moonless rainy night is not present, close your eyes, see blackness. So, faults disappear forever.

78.   Whenever your attention alights, At this very point, Experience.

79. Focus on fire rising through your form From the toes up Until the body burns to ashes But not you.

80. Meditate On the make believe world As burning to ashes, And become being above human.

81. As, subjectively, letters flow into words and words into sentences, and as, objectively, circles flow into worlds and worlds into principles, find at last these converging in our being.

82. Feel: my thought, I-ness, internal organs me.

83. Before desire And before knowing, How can I say I am? Consider. Dissolve in the beauty.

84. Toss attachment for body aside, Realizing I am everywhere. One who is everywhere is joyous.

85. Thinking no thing Will limited-self unlimit.

86. Suppose you contemplate Something beyond perception, Beyond grasping, Beyond not being you.

87. I am existing. This is mine. This is this. O, beloved, even in such know illimitably.

88. Each thing is perceived through knowing. The self shines in space through knowing. Perceive one being as knower and known.

89. Beloved, At this moment, Let mind, knowing, breath, form, Be included.

90. Touching eyeballs as a feather, Lightness between them opens into the heart And there permeates the cosmos.

91. Kind Devi, Enter etheric presence Pervading far above and below your form.

92. Put mindstuff in such inexpressible fineness Above, below and in your heart.

93. Consider any area of your present form As limitlessly spacious.

94. Feel your substance, Bones, flesh, blood, Saturated with cosmic essence.

95. Feel the fine qualities of creativity Permeating your breasts And assuming delicate configurations.

96. Abide in some place endlessly spacious, Clear of trees, hills, habitations. Thence comes the end of mind pressures.

97. Consider the plenum To be your own body of bliss.

98. In any easy position Gradually pervade an area between the armpits Into great peace.

99. Feel yourself as pervading all directions, Far, near.

100. The appreciation of objects and subjects Is the same for an enlightened As for an unenlightened person. The former has one greatness: He remains in the subjective mood, Not lost in things.

101. Believe omniscient, omnipotent, pervading.

102. Imagine spirit simultaneously Within and around you Until the entire universe spiritualizes.

103. With your entire consciousness In the very start of desire, of knowing, know.

104. O Shakti, Each particular perception is limited, Disappearing in omnipotence.

105. In truth forms are inseparate. Inseparate are omnipresent being And your own form. Realize each as made of this consciousness.

106. Feel the consciousness of each person As your own consciousness. So, leaving aside concern for your self, Become each being.

107. This consciousness exists as each being, And nothing else exists.

108. This consciousness is the spirit of guidance Of each one. Be this one.

109. Suppose your passive form to be an empty room With walls of skin empty.

110. Gracious One, play. The universe is an empty shell Wherein your mind frolics infinitely.

111. Sweet heartened One, Meditate on knowing and not-knowing, Existing and non-existing. Then leave both aside that you may be.

112. Enter space, supportless, eternal, still.

***

For the complete understanding of all of these *sutras* it is imperative to study in detail: Osho, *The Book of the Secrets*, vols. 1-5, St. Martin's Griffin, 1998.

We can only repeat here that in every *sutra* a way to recognize existence as divine consciousness is revealed, and divine consciousness as existence, to become aware of existence, to make a conscious attempt to learn to live and function consciously in all the aspects of existence, because this divine consciousness is our consciousness we use now in our life and work. It is our essence or soul. By recognizing our own consciousness of the soul we recognize consciousness as existence and existence as consciousness. It is all one and the same divine consciousness. This way we make existence soulful, creative and good. It already possesses all of these attributes, but wishes to become all of that through us. That is why it manifested itself into cosmos.

HOW CAN WE BE PERFECT

Be perfect, therefore, as your heavenly Father is perfect.
(Matthew, 5.48)

The only way for us to be perfect is to understand our position. In our body and mind we are on the most extreme opposition (Omega) point of the manifested existence. We should not stretch it any further while still being fascinated by our image in the mirror of existence, but should rather turn inwardly to get to know ourselves. Once we are the way we should be, then it will be our reflection in the mirror. Existence is a reflection of our being.

All the manifested universe was the act of movement of the consciousness from the divine source (Alpha) to its most distant opposition (Omega) point, to the man asking a question 'Who am I?'

The only correct way is the return to oneself, to its divine source through self-knowing, becoming aware of the higher dimensions which are actually our inner dimensions.

The circle of divine manifestation starts with the external manifestations of cosmos, and ends within the man.

The circling of divine consciousness is depicted with the well-known symbol of *Tai Chi*, or *yin* and *yang*. This symbol originates from the Slav-Aryan culture, the oldest one of its kind was found in the Balkans, in the ancient Vincan culture, and is nowadays wrongly attributed to Chinese philosophy. Although it is well-known, it is often falsely represented, turned upside down in all sorts of ways. This is the only correct representation of the symbol.

Tai chi represents the wholeness of existence and its perfection in the form of a circle, that is circling. It consists of the two fields of white and black, where the white symbolizes the principle of consciousness and black one the decline into oblivion of the unconscious. Likewise, of the two points, the first or the upper one marks the source of divine consciousness (Alpha) and the second or the lower one (Omega) its ultimate contrary position. The first point, black in the white field, signifies the principle of the 'divine particle', its original manifestation of the Absolute into its opposition, and the second one point, white in the black field, signifies awakening of the divine consciousness in its ultimate opposition state of the manifested world, into the body and mind, awakening of consciousness (white) in the unconsciousness (black). After this awakening the return to the divine source begins, the growth of the white field, of the consciousness, through man. The white field in its supreme realization contains the black point also, signifying the experience of awakening of the oppositions, of all the possibilities of existence. Fields and points are mixed so as to mimic the principle of circling of divine consciousness from its source (Alpha) to its ultimate opposition point (Omega) and the return to the original state.[33] This

---

[33] From this same principle the esoteric symbolics of Christ as Alpha and Omega originated. It is the symbolics of divine consciousness in its dynamic form, through manifestation. It is the deepest significance of Christ as the son of god. The descending of the Holy Spirit into the body is in the *Tai Chi* symbol represented with the black field that descends from the divine source all the way to the body, mind and ego. Resurrection is represented with the ascension of the white

mixed state reflects the holographic principle and time-lessness, it does not happen only over a period of time, but exists timelessly being always fully realized.

Divine Absolute

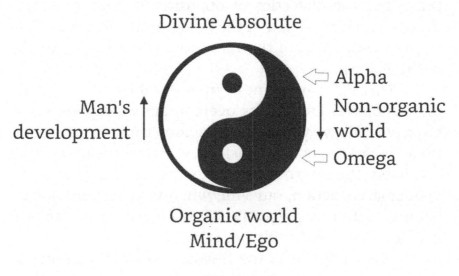

Man's development

Alpha
Non-organic world
Omega

Organic world
Mind/Ego

Picture 4

However, this most distant (Omega) point of divine manifestation is a very strange phenomenon. Its nature should be understood properly. It is this situation of ours. It can only be overcome by being understood properly.

On the one hand, it is the most supreme creativity of human consciousness, reflected in the creation of a human being ('in our image') which is also conscious and can have a will of its own, independent of the divine source. The peak of creativity is free will, the freedom of everything that could be, that could happen. It has two aspects: the first one is the freedom to know everything, and the other one is all the unwanted consequences of

field to the divine source. Everything else is theology that has a sole purpose of deceiving people.

such a freedom, all the negative experiences and pheno-mena. They have the complete freedom to take place. If they did not have that, it would not be real freedom. Nor would it be the real creativity. Still, chaos is not in charge there, but the dialectics of oppositions, because every-thing is interconnected in the holographic universe. Neg-ative phenomena are the measure of temptation of the positive ones.

This ultimate point of manifestation of the divine into its opposition and its overcoming we experience in ourselves always when we resist something negative and turn toward the positive instead, when we resist the urge and habit, the external impulse, when we strengthen our own creative action, our will; when we stop consciously before reacting impulsively. We try it out every time we should understand a thing or two.

We always have the freedom to act, the choice to turn to good or evil, constructive and positive, or destruc-tive and negative. This choice is neither random, nor ac-cidental, but it has the function of maturing the con-sciousness of itself. To the degree we are aware of us and our soul, we will choose good and constructive actions. To the degree we are unaware of ourselves and our sus-ceptibility is increased toward the outer influences, urges and habitual actions, we will exert a negative and de-structive influence on the surroundings.

This opposition creates dialectics that crystallizes the higher consciousness, the consciousness of the soul, which is not of the body and the conditioned mind but predates them.

Every moment of our life consists of these tempta-tions, and so do all our incarnations in the human body. All the ethics and religions, all the culture and science are composed of understanding these temptations.

To use a picturesque metaphor: from the divine source consciousness manifested itself in all ways possible as cosmos in all the dimensions (black field). When it reached its ultimate opposition point, within the alienated mind/ego of man, limited by the senses and the body, it must recognize itself there. The highest recognizes itself in what is lowest. In this breaking point the karmic drama of individual souls takes place, in the form of our human lives. It is based on one thing only: how to surpass impulses of the external influences – momentum of the first half of the circling of divine consciousness from the source and on to the outward swing, which happens spontaneously – and how to strengthen the force of the consciousness of itself. The first (black) half of the circle is spontaneous. It represents all the impulsive nature we see that is driven by the force of its own laws and instincts. It is the entire outer world. The other half (white) of the circle leading upward, to the source of the divine, happens through man, through human self-knowing. His self-knowing is practically reduced to understanding the outer nature and its laws (science) and resisting its impulses in our being, body and our actions (ethics), giving way to the consciousness itself and its will, instead. Understanding unconscious impulses means gaining power and command over them. It is symbolized by the fact that the black field has a white dot inside, the principle of consciousness. Consciousness awakens in the unconsciousness. However, black field of the unconscious still prevails, conditioning the consciousness. In the end, the white field has a black dot inside, consciousness contains within itself all the experience of the unconscious and governs it.

Resisting one's impulses must be based on understanding why it is a good idea to do it, on the consciousness itself, never on the forced division of will which always creates a new opposition. Understanding is the only thing that awakens and uplifts us, it is the factor that unites everything and not the one that drives a wedge between. The reason for this is that our own consciousness must be the only attractive force in our sublimation toward the divine source. Nothing else. Nothing that is of this, outer world, can be this because it all belongs to the first part of the circle, the spontaneous nature which manifests itself. The only one who will turn to the divine is the one who abandoned everything and who is abandoned by everything.

The complete understanding of this circling and shift which happens in man was presented in the science of yoga, in the work *Yoga Sutras* by Patanjali. Understanding the outer nature and its relationship toward consciousness was put forth in the science of *sâmkhya*, the practice of yoga is based upon. Yoga is actually meditation, the turning of consciousness toward its own source, the turning of man toward the consciousness of his soul. In this science it was described how man could understand his inner nature and come in terms with his outer nature, which is known as ethics, or *yama* and *niyama* in the works of Patanjali. The key turning of consciousness toward its source and resisting the outer impulses and influences is called *pratyahara*. The practitioners of meditation describe this with words that the consciousness should always be kept at the doors of its perception, never crossing over the doorstep. Then, man uplifts to the divine consciousness of his soul. In such a manner, man becomes perfect like his creator - the divine consciousness. It was also described in the biblical myth of heaven, the exile from Eden and the return to it, when we will be like gods. However, that was and still is a myth, with no practice to make it happen.

The reality is that it is not enough to philosophize about it, or believe in it, or pray for it. One should be that with his/her entire being. It is possible because we never were outside it, nor could we ever be outside the divine consciousness, we are always in it, and, truthfully, we are itself. All it takes for us to do is to make the unconscious conscious.

Ethical preparation for this reversal has been developing throughout the entire existence of human culture, thinking and comprehension of the world on a collective level. Comprehension of the consciousness of the soul began with Plato and Socrates, everything is already explained there, but more through images and hints, through the culture of dialogue, which back then in the unconscious world was more than necessary, much like it is today. At least 90% of evil and violence in this world could be avoided if any good will for dialogue and understanding of what was really going on were present.

Round about that time Patanjali wrote *Yoga Sutras*, which are actually much older. The same issue is debated in a far more precise manner and based on scientific grounds. Yoga or meditation is a science in the works of Patanjali. There are no stories or descriptions, merely instructions for the practice that are so accurate that the only person who can recognize and understand them is the one who applies them on himself/herself.

Buddhism developed from the practice of meditation, as a direct path to divine consciousness, but as an individual path, for each man individually who is mature enough to go back to the source. The path of Buddhism is a direct exit from time of existing in illusion, and is not aimed toward collective application in time. To an individual man the exit from the game of illusion is offered, it is not intended for the entire human society that stays in this world to play the game all the way through. Buddhism therefore serves as the much needed beacon. The light of the consciousness of the soul is preserved in it and each person can recognize it for himself/herself.

The consciousness of the soul that acts in this world, and is tied to the divine, manifested itself through Jesus Christ. That is why his destiny was a lot more dramatic than Buddha's. He showed what it is like to be crucified between divine and human, between the first, descending and the second, ascending phase of the circling of divine consciousness within itself. His instructions given during the *Sermon on the Mount* are a great beacon for human souls in this world. In the *Gospel of Thomas* they are even more so. The most important instruction is for us to be as wise as serpents and as innocent as doves. Snake is the symbol of materiality and the descending trajectory of consciousness, and dove is the symbol of the consciousness of the soul following the ascending path. They should be united in this world. Nothing portrays the human position in this world like the ultimate opposition points of the manifestation of existence, like a man crucified on the cross, between the vertical leading toward the divine and the earthly horizontal. Its position on the cross is the best depiction of the position of man through whom the manifestation of the divine crosses paths, whether it will exist aware of itself or not, whether it will resurrect from the manifested nature, the declining path, and rise up to the divine source.

The human society has grasped all of this wrongly and literally, and has been doing so, for such a long time, people imitated by praying to the symbol of the cross, they turned everything into a ritual performed with a hand in the shape of a cross, whilst at the same time burning at the stake anyone who dared think otherwise, or more precisely anyone who tried to make a sense of it all.

In more recent times, the understanding of ethics with which the reversal of the ultimate opposition point through man is made in the correct way, was introduced by the philosopher Immanuel Kant in his work *The Critique of Practical Reason.*[34] He says: *Two things fill the mind with ever new and increasing admiration and awe, the more often and steadily we reflect upon them: the starry heavens above me and the moral law within me. I do not seek or conjecture either of them as if they were veiled obscurities or extravagances beyond the horizon of my vision; I see them before me and connect immediately with the consciousness of my existence.* Never have more beautiful words been used to express this shift in consciousness of the human mind, this ultimate opposition point of the divine, from the descending path to the ascension. The word *critique* in the title of his work denotes the limitations of the mind, what the mind can do with itself, and what it cannot, what its true role is. Too much blood has been shed throughout the entire human history for us to be able to reach this understanding. By the way, who bothers to read Kant, Plato, Schelling today? Only the students who have to.

What Kant correctly anticipated connecting the consciousness of his soul with the starry heaven, has become clear to us only with the development of physics, which has brought us to the understanding in its best and final reach of the universe as a hologram. Since universe is a hologram with us as its conscious subjects, a look to

---

[34] Immanuel Kant: The Critique of Practical Reason.

the starry sky fills us with the greatest rapture like we looked in our own soul, in the embodiment of divine. Mature souls, such as Kant's was, connect the dots straight away.

The same principle of hologram gives the universal ethical principle that connects us to the divine. This holographic principle is as follows: do (not) unto others what you do (not) want done unto you. The same holographic principle is a part of the Delphi oracle: *Know thyself, and thou wilt know the world and God.*

As we gradually become aware of our higher dimensions, through meditation and the out-of-body experiences meditation brings along, we become aware of the dimensions of existence itself, because they are in us. Those higher dimensions are analogue to the higher consciousness and increased connectedness within the holographic unity, a greater understanding of the world and enhanced empathy with the overall life. For example, higher consciousness of the higher dimensions we develop by avoiding to react straight away to some stimulus or challenge, but rather wait, sleep on it, because morning is always wiser that the evening, and only then we choose to react. This uplifts us from the physical plane, where everything is separate in space and time (picture 1), where cause and consequence are expressed in their ultimate outcome only, and we learn to connect to the consciousness of the higher realms where space and time are relative, where everything has a wider context and clearer connectedness. Our reaction where we halt and wait first, react with an insight, generate a creative action, full of understanding and reconciliation, bringing forth the solution to the problems. The faster we react, the more unconsciously we act, creating and multiplying a bundle of problems needlessly in the process. The very power of restraining instincts and impulses for spontaneous reaction strengthens our consciousness and our ability to rise up to the higher dimensions. The practice of meditation consists of that discipline alone, of being able to restrain the bodily and mental reactions and uplifting ourselves to the higher consciousness where everything is a lot clearer. For this reason meditation is practiced with the stillness of the body and mind. All spiritual disciplines possess a certain method of restraint. Until we stop with the spontaneous expressions we cannot turn toward ourselves and ascend. *Stillness in meditation corresponds with the moment of stillness when the divine consciousness reaches the ultimate opposition point in the manifestation of existence after which it changes its direction upward, to its divine source.*

All of it is readily available here and now, we occasionally manifest and experience all of it, and that inspires and attracts us the most in our everyday life. All it takes is to turn it into a fine culture of demeanor and actions. So as not to remain only abstract philosophy or blind faith and conviction. This type of culture has always existed in this world, we should simply become aware of it. It is yoga or the science of meditation, put forth in the Patanjali's work of *Yoga Sutras*. The Buddhist practice expands it in all the details. *I Ching* gives us connection with the higher mind and consciousness of the soul.

The ultimate opposition point is the expression of the ultimate freedom of existence. It is rock bottom existence, it is every picture of hell we have in this world, but the greatest potential for the turning point, as well. Anyone who hit his/her lowest point in life became a better man/woman.

If the shift does not happen in the right way, through man and his correctness, through his perfecting himself in order to become the embodiment of perfection, than this same freedom that gives him the possibility of return to the divine, gives him power of ultimate destruction – and destruction is nothing but turning the consciousness toward some other side, and not back to its source, through man.

This phenomenon is very simple and logical. When the manifestation of divine consciousness reaches its ultimate opposition point, in the human body and mind, at the same time it obtains the ultimate freedom of action. It obtains the freedom so as to choose of its own the return to the original divine state, to be able to recognize the omnipresence of divine. A conscious individual must of its own will choose the return to the divine, and he chooses that by recognizing divine in everything. Divine alone is no longer capable of returning to itself once it forms into a self-conscious individual, man, it cannot move further from the ultimate opposition point. Predominance of the unconscious (black field) is at its peak then. The only consciousness (white dot in the black field) that appears in man is his mind and ego, his individual will. Only from the individual consciousness of man the return to the divine source starts. If divine consciousness itself had the power to orchestrate this shift, nothing new would ever happen, it would not be the free will of humans, consciousness in it would not experience the ultimate opposition point and its purpose which is to serve as the reference point of the final differentiation of consciousness in the mirror of existence.

If this same freedom can in its freedom and naive delight of its newly found individuality turn **to the other side, it may continue to stretch the opposition (Omega)** *point further than what the body and life were previously envisaged for. Further away than God anticipated. The perfect circling of Tai Chi falls apart then. Consequently, all the evil and destruction take place.* This is the perfect definition of evil. Evil is simply going further than what is sufficient, trying out more than necessary, repeating experiences once too often than what is enough. It is, in a nutshell, redundant. Evil is something that is not needed for man, life or the world. But in the perfect freedom of everything to get itself manifested, that, too, has a freedom to manifest. This is the perfect illustration of the perfection of existence.

Actually, *the consciousness of the soul can never divert to the other side, further away from the Omega point.* It always moves the way it is shown in picture 4. It can always go back to its original divine source because it is no different from it. What would happen to the human being if in his insanity he went beyond the Omega point? The consciousness of the soul would leave him and he would like an organic portal go on moving along the lines of inertia of the material, physical mind while he still can, with an even growing destruction along the way. The world would be ruled by the heartless non-humans fighting nature and people continuously. Does that sound familiar?

This exaggeration is something people do until they learn that through this they only lose the consciousness of their soul, the nature of reality, to a sufficient degree to be able to make the right turning toward divine, the return to oneself and their authenticity. Any other direction would signify waste of energy and deceiving the consciousness. Those two represent the essence of human slavery.

Stretching the ultimate opposition point away from the perfect circling is like stretching an elastic band, we strengthen that what we resist. We try out all the negative states with this, but at the same time we strengthen the energy to be able to go back. The ultimate opposition point must have its kinetic energy for pulling back, and this energy is received from the movement in the opposite direction of that of the return, away from the perfect circle, like with stretching the elastic band. Practically speaking, by trying out the mistakes we strengthen the awareness of what is right, experiencing all the wrong paths until we find the one that is right, after enough cognition of the outward, we turn toward the inner values. At the same time it is the turning point in the cycle of incarnations when we are done with gathering experiences and we turn to the consciousness of the soul.

We do not experience the stretching of the ultimate opposition point simply by encountering evil and negativity. We also try it out by creating all those things that are not evil, but are, neither the reflection of divine, and those are all the things people in this world learn to be able to work and create, the causes and consequences, all the arts and sciences. All the engineering and buildings and the things we see as human creations, small and big, necessary and needless, the creative ones and complete trash. Man uses all of that to perfect his awareness of what is right and what is wrong, of the reality in which he lives, of his relationship toward reality and the world, of himself.

Basically, consciousness is the only force that can put a stop to evil. Stopping the redundant movement from the ultimate (Omega) point, into needless and destructive, only consciousness is able to perform, to correct the movement to the right direction, because only consciousness acts on the second, ascending half of the circling of divine, after the most distant point. Only consciousness can turn life from the most remote point to the proper return toward divine, by understanding the entire process.

In the first (black) half of manifestation the mechanical forces of nature act. On the second (white) only the consciousness inspired by the divine source acts, with the perfection it originated from. *It acts through man only*. Having shaped the man into existence, the nature has finished its job and now everything is up to him. The nature has finished setting the stage, which is life on planet Earth. People now together with their souls play their parts, the karmic dramas, and they all together play the mystery drama of the great awakening.

Only by the proper practice of meditation we harmonize with the manifested consciousness of the divine and its circling within itself, only with meditation we harmonize perfectly with the movement of the Omega point upward in the direction of the source, we harmonize with Tao, or the "heaven's way".[35]

With meditation the life energy is harmonized, *chi*. The ideal circling of energy is depicted in the *Tai Chi* symbol. In the human body life energy moves from the first to the last chakra, through the seven phases, conditioning all the states of consciousness in man. The upper point, Alpha, represents the top chakra, *sahasrara*, and the lowest point, Omega, the first chakra, *muladhara*. Having raised awareness of our own being in meditation, we automatically correct the movement of all the psycho-

---

[35] All that is required for the practice of meditation can be found in my book "Meditation – The First and the Last Step – From Understanding to Practice".

energy flows of our being and the overall existence, we stop the movement away from the most remote Omega point, where it would be needless and destructive. In our being it is practically applied with the cessation of energy consumption through the lower points, which becomes manifested in the form of excessive sexuality, aggressiveness and ambition, egocentricity and vanity. When owing to the mature insight we stop wasting energy on the activity of the lower chakras, they automatically rise upward, along the white field of consciousness, through our entire being all the way to the top Alpha point, to *sahasrara*. That is how we become perfect.

Our being is designed in such a way to orchestrate this entire process perfectly, its energy has a natural tendency to move comprehensively because it is a reflection of the wholeness of the being. All we have to do is refrain from interfering with it with our little unconscious mind. That is the reason why in meditation the mind is transcended, overcome, calmed.

By transcending the mind we get acquainted with the higher dimensions of our own being and existence itself. At the beginning of the book we stated that we do not see that everything is perfect because we do not see the entire nature, all its dimensions and the entire process of causality that extends across all the dimensions. Now we see how such sighting is achieved. By knowing the higher dimensions we see the causes we could not see before, we see causes in past lives, not merely this current one, the causes that elude our sensory perception. Once we are in possession of the complete insight, we see that everything is perfect.

Even without meditation in every man the testing of the final stretching point happens, the exact point where turning toward oneself and consciousness takes place, where unconscious reactions stop, and conscious actions begin. But then the testing of this final reach gets a lot rougher, those are all the karmic dramas and the suffering of man, everything we experience in our everyday life. Throughout all our lives.

Reaching the turning point, the Omega point and the correct passing through its phase toward consciousness and Alpha point, depends on the karmic maturity of our incarnation cycle and consciousness. One and the same consciousness of the soul we use in all our incarnations for all our experiences. With meditation we alert and strengthen this one and the same consciousness, the consciousness of our soul. Its awakening speeds up (compresses) the time of maturing of karmic experiences of existence and reaching the turning point. It does not mean we have to wait for our karmic maturity at the end of the incarnation cycle, in order to go through the Omega point properly. We should just become aware of it. By becoming aware we remove the time, we speed up the whole process so that its outcome is always possible. The door to freedom is always open, we were simply pushing on the wrong side, forward, and it opens when we pull it toward us. While we were guided by our unconscious mind we were always looking outside, fascinated by the objects and contents. It was the reason why without the karmic drama, without going down the wrong paths we failed to reach the only one which is right, the awareness of the need to meditate.

Experiencing the ultimate reach of freedom to be unconscious is a way for us to become conscious. All our wandering through the valley of tears and suffering stops the moment we consciously do away with unconscious reactions, when the person remains calm and composed because of the clear insight into the nature of events. Our entire existence prior to that point was dominated by unconscious reactions, they were the chains of our slavery. This chain was made up of two types of links: of attachment and repulsion (of desires and hate). Both yielded disastrous results and suffering. By attaining the consciousness of testifying or the transcendental consciousness, we do not give up on events, as it may appear to an inexperienced critic, we give up on the unconscious reactions thus achieving psychological objectivity regarding those events; avoiding to react spontaneously we enable ourselves with a clear vision of reality, seeing it for what it really is, and act accordingly, harmonizing ourselves with reality and divine consciousness. That is, after all, the essence of human culture or, at least, it should be. When we see events for what they really are, we then return the awareness of them directly to God through our soul, and then we are able to act with divine consciousness. It is a moment when the ultimate opposition point Omega, our mind/ego, fulfills its true purpose, it stops unconsciously moving on to the opposite, needless and negative, and starts to rise upward, to the white field, to harmonize with the divine consciousness, and then it draws up the perfect *yin* and *yang* circle.

There are two ways we can harmonize with the reality: nolens volens, willing or unwilling. Willing harmonization is when we consciously harmonize with reality by means of our own awakening, by meditation. Unwilling is when we are forced to do it by reality itself, during the painful process of breaking up our illusions because we can never, in any way possible, be outside the divine.

Such is the nature of freedom, it does not have any hypocritical morality or any rules of the standard kind, it is always freedom for everything possible, in favor of something and against something, alike. That is why it is so pure and direct. That is why the freedom of all kinds of actions and inactions is so inviting to young souls.

All it takes is to recognize the same freedom of divine consciousness that conditions everything in our freedom of choice. We should not alter anything, we should simply increase the awareness of everything we do. The objective reality itself will change everything we do wrong to right, it will give us the right choice. It is not possible to do something wrong with the full awareness. It is so because consciousness is a direct expression of the perfection of existence, which consciousness is because it is the creator of existence; consciousness is at the base of existence. It is this consciousness we do everything with. For that reason it is impossible to act consciously against existence itself.

Can you resist all the petty temptations that keep you trapped with their constructs, and have been doing it for so long and so skillfully that you have learnt to enjoy them, to find all sorts of justification for them?

When will you begin?

Everything can be done now, and only now.

Now is the perfect moment.

Even if you are a little late, do not worry.

Perfection will not suffer for it.

For the divine consciousness you are perfect exactly as you are, every moment of every day.

Made in United States
North Haven, CT
01 December 2022

27619955R00143